RICHMONDS OF THE WORLD

RICH TAPESTRY OF RICHMONDS AS THE MOST NAMED PLACE ON EARTH

BARCLAY SIMPSON

Published by Barclay Simpson 2013

ISBN 978-1-78222-108-1

Front cover photo: Mike Kipling.

Book design, layout and production management by Into Print
www.intoprint.net
+44 (0)1604 832149
Printed and bound in UK, Australia and USA by Lightning Source

CONTENTS

FOREWORD

Growing up in Richmond, I remember being proud of the fact that it was the very first town in the world to be called Richmond, but I don't think I was aware there were quite so many others of the same name.

Looking back, I am not sure that I truly appreciated everything the market town of Richmond has to offer, with its friendly people, natural beauty, Norman castle, Georgian theatre, impressive architecture and cobbled marketplace. Or how lucky I was to grow up surrounded by stunning views and living next to the powerful River Swale (that came into our cellar when it flooded!) with its magnificent waterfall.

I do recall being fascinated by local folklore, with tales of Alan the Red, and being horrified by the tale of the little Drummer Boy who suddenly stopped drumming in an underground tunnel between Richmond and Easby.

I now realise how lucky I was to grow up in Richmond, and recognise what a sense of community there is. Its residents work hard to ensure that Richmond, North Yorkshire, remains unique, from the reopening of the Georgian Theatre Royal in the 1960s, to the 2007 launch of The Station - a wonderful cinema, cafe and arts centre with artisan food producers - in the historic railway station, where the last train left in 1969!

Richmond, North Yorkshire is a very special place and I urge you to appreciate it if you live there and come and explore it if you don't. And to all the residents of the other places named after this one, I hope you have the good fortune to share the values and the beauty of the very first Richmond!

AMANDA BERRY OBE

British Academy of Film and Television Arts

The British Film Academy was initiated during 1947 by directors Sir Alexander Korda, David Lean, Roger Manvell, Laurence Olivier, Emeric Pressburger, Michael Powell, Carol Reed (later Sir Carol Reed), and other major people of the British movie industry. During 1958, the Academy merged with the Guild of Television Producers and Directors to form the Society of Film and Television Arts, which eventually became the British Academy of Film and Television Arts during 1976.

BAFTA is an independent charity with a mission to "support, develop and promote the art forms of the moving image, by identifying and rewarding excellence, inspiring practitioners and benefiting the public". They have frequently received funding from the National Lottery as well as giving funding to British educational institutions. In addition to high-profile awards ceremonies BAFTA manages a year-round programme of educational events including movie screenings, tribute evenings, interviews, lectures and debates with major industry people. BAFTA is funded by a membership of about 6500 people from the movie, television and video game industries. BAFTA's main headquarters is on Piccadilly in London, but it also has regional offices in Scotland, in Wales, in New York and in Los Angeles.

These four parts of the Academy operated initially with their own brands (BAFTA Scotland, BAFTA Cymru, BAFTA East Coast and BAFTA Los Angeles). During July 2010, all parts of the Academy were brought together as one fully affiliated BAFTA. The Academy's awards are in the form of a theatrical mask designed by American sculptor Mitzi Cunliffe, which was commissioned by the Guild of Television Producers and Directors during 1955. It has since become an internationally-recognised symbol.

During November 2007 a special tribute programme was shown on ITV in the UK celebrating 60 years of the organisation named 'Happy Birthday BAFTA'.

The Academy has been associated with the British monarchy since Prince Philip, Duke of Edinburgh became the British Film Academy's first president during the 1940s. The Earl Mountbatten of Burma and The Princess Royal have since had this position, and during 2010 Prince William became the newest Academy president. Amanda has been CEO since 1999 and transformed the organisation into dynamic force for industry.

RICHMOND

Richmond, the capital of Swaledale, was the first town in world called this name: *Swale* came from the Danish name 'Suales' meaning fast-flowing and the River Swale is fastest in England. In the 9th century, the Danes came via Ireland, the Isle of Man and the Lake District. Originally called Hindrelac, Richmond was mentioned in the Doomsday Book (which is held at the National Archives in Kew): Hindrelac is an Anglo-Viking name thought to describe a woodland clearing frequented by a hind or female deer. The present name of this historic Swaledale town is Old French and derives from Riche-Monte, a common French place name which means strong hill. It was here in 1071 that a French Count called Alan the Red (Rufus) of Brittany built a castle on the lofty hill overlooking the River Swale. Alan was a Breton and he and his Knights had come from St Aubin du Cormier in Brittany. *Coincidentally there are, 57 communities called St Aubin in France. A Castle was built at St Aubin du Cormier to much same design as Richmond in about 1170 but is now a ruin.*

William the Conqueror's strategy of Harrowing the North from 1069 – 1070 AD was an act of genocide, that became known as the Harrying of the North. From the Humber to the Tees, William's men burnt whole villages and slaughtered the inhabitants. Food stores and livestock were destroyed so that anyone surviving the initial massacre would succumb to starvation over the winter. The land was salted to destroy its productivity for decades forward, survivors reduced to cannibalism. Contemporary biographers of William considered it to be his cruellest act and a stain upon his soul, but the deed was not mainstream knowledge before Whig history. In his Ecclesiastical History the Doomsday Anglo-Norman chronicler Orderic Vitalis, said: *'The King stopped at nothing to hunt his enemies. He cut down many people and destroyed homes and land. Nowhere else had he shown such cruelty. This made a real change. To his shame, William made no effort to control his fury, punishing the innocent with the guilty. He ordered that crops and herds, tools and food be burned to ashes.'* More than 100,000 people perished of hunger: because of the scorched earth policy, much of the land was laid waste and depopulated, a fact to which the Doomsday Book, written almost two decades later, readily attests.

'I, William the Bastard give and grant thee Alan my nephew ear Earldom of Bretagne and his heirs for ever all the time and lands which lately has been Earl Edwin of Yorkshire with fees and all privilege and confirm as free and honourable member from the grave of honour of Richmond to Alan Rufus from King William.' (Quote: Display at Richmond Castle)

The territory surrounding Richmond became Alan the Red's land and was known as Richmond Shire, a Shire comprised of the former Viking districts of Gilling and Hang. Alan the Red also built a castle at Middleham in Wensleydale, which belonged to his brother Ribald. Like William the Conqueror, Alan Rufus died an incredibly rich man; in adjusting his fortune to modern standards by accounting for inflation, it is likely that the man was worth an equivalent of $178.65 billion [dollars or pounds??], mainly originating from the 250,000 acres of land bestowed upon him by the new King of England for his cooperation in the invasion. This figure puts him as one of the richest people in human history.

George Calvert, Founder of Maryland and first Lord of Baltimore came from Kiplin Hall, Richmond; Francis Nicholson from Downholme Park, Richmond, was another Founder. They had many achievements in new world: they left a legacy of designing the road system for the now capital of Maryland, Annapolis, the layout of the town of Williamsburg and also set up the college of William and Mary in Maryland.

Subsequent Lords of Richmondshire were known as the Earls of Richmond and included King Henry VII. In 1499, four years after his coronation, King Henry, the Earl of Richmond, constructed a palace at a place called Sheen in the county of Surrey. Sheen was re-named Richmond, taking its name from its Yorkshire predecessor. The now famous London Borough of Richmond upon Thames has developed from this. Following this renaming, 'Richmonds' spread around Globe.

Richmonds of the World (ROW)

With the coming of the internet we are now able to keep in touch more closely with other Richmonds. In the 1980s a global Richmond network was set up: the Mayor of Richmond, North Yorkshire, Roy Cross produced a leaflet featuring all the Richmonds around the world, which in 1980 he sent to all the other Richmonds. The ROW Concept was the also an idea of Councillor Serge Lourie, Leader of Richmond Council, Surrey, and Rick Tatnell of Richmond, Virginia with the purpose of linking all towns and cities named Richmond and encouraging mutual co-operation and international friendships.

- For the 2000 Millennium, Graham Walker and Dennys Clarkson (Richmond, North Yorkshire) produced a pictorial calendar that they sent to Richmond settlements around the World.
- In 2007, Jamestown Virginia celebrated its 400th birthday as the Founding settlement in Virginia and the USA. Serge Lourie, then Leader of Richmond upon Thames Council with a party of 20, (including Jason Debney based in Richmond Park and working for Thames Landscape Strategy) went to the fabulous 2-week celebrations.
- 2008 saw a Richmonds of the World meeting at Richmond University, London. Delegates from Richmond Virginia and Richmond Council came with idea of encouraging mutual co-operation and international friendships with all other Richmonds; Serge Lourie (then leader of Council) welcomed Rick Tatnall from Virginia
- In 2008 there was also a ROW photographic exhibition (commissioned by Richmond London Arts Service) displayed in the Old Town Hall, Richmond upon Thames.
- Summer2009 had the exhibition travelling to *The Station*, Richmond, North Yorkshire where it was a great success with 12 pages of complimentary comments; 11,000 people saw exhibition. Four representatives from Richmond, London came to the opening where they met Mayor Gillson and William Hague (present MP for Richmond, Yorkshire for 20 years). *The Station* won a National Rail Heritage Award for its conversion from a dilapidated building into a venue that includes a 2-screen cinema, restaurant, shops, education centre, art gallery and meeting rooms
- May 2012 saw 8 people from Richmond, Virginia attend the New Mayor of Richmond Ceremony- making in Richmond Town Hall in Yorkshire and where they were a given rousing reception.
- Councillor Barrie Heap and present Town Crier. Mayor 2010 -11 above [Does this refer to a picture??]

- On September 15 2012, I attended with Sheila Wilkinson from Richmond marketing the 25th Great River Race where over 300 boats of all sizes and class compete to row the 20 miles from Canary Wharf, London to Ham House, and Richmond upon Thames. I met the present Mayor of Richmond Rita Palmer and her consort. It was a wonderful event enjoyed by all and graced by good weather *[BS]*. The 2013 Great River Race will be held on September 7.
- On the very same day as the Great River Race. Richmond, London were playing Richmond, Yorkshire at cricket match in very beautiful Yorkshire weather.
- On October 20, 2012, Paul Pasquale (famous Richmond, Virginia sculptor) and Steve Edge (Artistic Director from Rogue Folk Club Vancouver) attended the Richmond Folk sing-along at Bishop Blaize Hotel and played some songs, as you can see from the picture, below.
- In April 15 2013, I met a barman working in the lovely Waterman's Arms in Richmond London who has said he had lived in Richmond, Queensland; in came a woman who joined the conversation and said she was born in Richmond, Melbourne; then through the door came the Richmond Folk Club - many who lived in Richmond, London – all talking to me, from Richmond Yorkshire! *[BS]*

Number of Richmonds around the World

Richmond has 55 places across the world named after it – more than any other major British place name: London has 46, Oxford 41, Manchester 36, Wellington 35, Bristol 35, Newcastle 29, and Plymouth 24.

- South Africa has 5 Richmonds, Jamaica and Australia 4, Grenada 2.
- The Bahamas, New Zealand, Trinidad and Tobago and St Vincent and the Grenadines all have one.
- There's a Richmond District in San Francisco and a Richmond Hill, Ontario.
- Fiji also has a Richmond Hill, which looks very peaceful
- Richmond Sri Lanka which is Second Richmond castle is and is a beautiful stately home where most on Presidents of Sri Lanka were educated. Richmonds in South Africa would be influence by Dukes of Richmond.
- Sri Lanka boasts the only other Richmond Castle. A stately home, it has been used as a learning establishment where many of the country's presidents have been educated.
- Richmond Heights, Vancouver in British Columbia took its name from the Duke of Richmond. Charles Lennox, 1st Duke of Richmond, 1st Duke of Lennox, 1st Duke of Aubigny (29 July 1672 – 27 May 1723) was the illegitimate son of Charles II and his mistress. He is an ancestor of Diana Princess of Wales, Camilla Duchess of Cornwall, and Sarah Duchess of York. *(Source: Wikipedia)*

There are over 2 million people who live in Richmonds around the World - to visit all 55 of them is a Herculean task; however, a start has been made:

- David Hodgson and Trevor Draper (Richmond, Yorkshire) have visited 12 Richmonds worldwide
- Walter Bear (Richmond, Melbourne) has visited 6
- Barclay Simpson visited 3 Richmonds in one day (London, Richmond area in Sheffield and Richmond, Yorkshire).

Some facts

- In 2013 The Georgian Theatre Royal in Richmond, North Yorkshire is 225 years old.
- Charles Dickens visited Richmond, Yorkshire and London and Turner has painted both locations. Turners original painting of Richmond castle is in V+A Museum London
- The Coast to Coast Walk (from St Bees to Whitby), classed as one of the best walks in the world, brings people from all over the globe through Richmond, Yorkshire. An arduous walk of over 170 miles, many do it in two halves but all come to Richmond.
- Richmond, London has 4m visitors annually: it has world-class attractions Hampton Court and Kew Gardens.
- Richmond upon Thames hosted some Olympic cycling Events in 2012. Henry VII and Queen Elizabeth 1 lived in this premier borough as do some of today's Royalty.
- Richmond Bridge in Tasmania is the oldest bridge in Australia, which was built by convicts.
- In 2021 Richmond Castle, Yorkshire will be celebrating its 950th birthday.

(Source: Wikipedia)

Many Richmonds around the world are very important centres of Government.

- Richmond, Virginia is very important town in the history of America and holds great importance with the Governance of Virginia. It is close to Washington and New York.
- Richmond, California played a very strategic role in World War 2 with boat production and is a major oil production town.
- Staten Island is where lot of people started their new life in the 19th century – and its original name is Richmond in Richmond County
- Vancouver is major city and held the winter Olympics in 2010 and some events were held Richmond Vancouver
- 3 Dukes of Richmond were Founders of Northern Richmonds in Maine Massachusetts, New Hampshire - beautiful locations - and founded the Canadian towns in Ontario and British Columbia.

When you visit the UK, please come to Richmond, Yorkshire where it all started in 1071 and be assured of a very warm welcome.

If you have any events ideas photos especially please send to: richmondsoftheworld@gmail.com

Enjoy Richmonds of the World!
Charles Barclay Simpson

Swaledale, Yorkshire, England. Photo: Mike Kipling.

RICHMOND, NORTH YORKSHIRE

A market town located on the edge of the Yorkshire Dales National Park Richmond is the administrative centre for the Richmondshire district. The River Swale which is third fastest river in the UK flows past the bottom of the Castle, one of the features which make Richmond a magnet for tourists. In 2009 Richmond was named UK Town of the Year. The Sunday Times March, 2013 listed Richmond in the Top 10 Towns in North of England to live and BBC Lonely Planet Magazine commented it was one of best secrets in world in April 2013.

Betty James (in the Rough Guide) wrote that *"Without any doubt Richmond is the most romantic place in the whole of the North East of England."*

Joseph E Morris agreed, although went further to say, *"Richmond is, beyond all question, the most romantic town in the North of England." (Source: Rough Guide)*

History – an overview

As mentioned in the preface, Richmond was founded in 1071 by the Breton Alan Rufus, on lands granted to him by William the Conqueror. It was a huge estate from Durham to London covering 11 counties including Yorkshire, Nottinghamshire, Lincolnshire, Cambridgeshire, Dorset, Hertfordshire, Norfolk and Suffolk.

Alain Le Roux (Alan the Red) had the Honour of Richmond and was given control of York. By 1086 Alain was one of the richest and most powerful men in England: he had received some 250,000 acres (1,000 km²) in land grants as a reward for his allegiance, totalling about £11,000 by the time of his death in 1093. This would make Alan Rufus the wealthiest Briton in all the history of the British Isles. His fortune was estimated to be equivalent to £81.33 billion in 2007.

The prosperity of the medieval market town and centre of the Swaledale wool industry greatly increased in the late 17th and 18th centuries with the burgeoning lead mining industry in nearby Arkengarthdale.

Europe's first gas works was built in the town in 1830. Richmond was one of first towns in the North to get gas street lighting.

Richmond Castle

Richmond Castle by Turner.

An imposing edifice overlooking the fast-flowing Swale, it is situated in the town centre and is a major tourist attraction. It has had a colourful history: Richmond was part of the lands of the Earldom of Richmond, which was intermittently held by the Dukes of Brittany, until the 14th century. In 1453, the Earldom was conferred on Edmund Tudor and became merged in the crown when Edmund's son Henry became king, as Henry VII in 1485.

- During the English Civil War, the Covenanter Army led by David Leslie, Lord Newark, took over the castle and conflict between local Catholics and Scottish Presbyterians ensued.
- There are stories that Robin Hood visited the Castle and another that Potter Thompson found King Arthur and his Knights sleeping in a cave under Richmond Castle and was so frightened as they began to wake, that he ran away. He tried for years afterward to find the cave again but never succeeded.
- During World War 1, the Castle served as a barracks for soldiers and 16 conscientious objectors were imprisoned there.
- There are now no traces of the barracks but the Keep is one of finest in the UK. It is over 100 feet high with walls 11 feet thick to hold the structure intact. Scolland's Hall is the gatehouse.
- Henry Jenkins, buried in Bolton-on-Swale Richmond, is said to have been 169 years old at his death. He claimed to have been born in 1501and died 1670. There is annual dinner to commemorate his life on the first Friday in October.

Middleham Castle

Although not in the town, here is an appropriate place to describe this Castle, also built by Alan Rufus in 1190. In 1270 Middleham Castle came into the hands of the Nevilles whose most notable member of was Richard Neville known to history as the "Kingmaker", a leading figure in the War of the Roses. Following the death of Richard Duke of York at Wakefield in December 1460, his younger sons, George Duke of Clarence and Richard Duke of Clarence, (twins) came into Warwick's care, and lived at Middleham with Warwick's own family. Their brother King Edward IV was imprisoned at Middleham for a short time, having been captured by Warwick in 1469. After Warwick's death at Barnet in 1471 and Edward's restoration to the throne, his brother Richard married Anne Neville (younger daughter of Warwick) and made Middleham his main home. Their son Edward was born at Middleham and later also died there. Richard ascended to the throne as King Richard III but spent little or no time at Middleham in his two-year reign. After Richard's death at Bosworth in 1485 the castle remained in royal hands until the reign of James 1, when it was sold. It fell into disuse and disrepair during the 17th Century. It was garrisoned during the Civil War but saw no action. The ruins are now in the care of English Heritage.

Photo: Moonburst.

Richmond Attractions

- The cobbled market place is one of the largest in England and of French design. Prince Charles calls Richmond the 'Siena of the North'. He was here in 2005 with the Duchess of Cornwall.
- Based in the old Trinity Church in the centre of the town's market place is The Green Howards Museum which narrates the story of this regiment. In 2012 it received funding to update and refurbish and new features should re-open to the public in November 2013.
- The town is also home to the Richmondshire Museum which features an 'All Creatures Great and Small' TV set and a Fenwicks' Store. The latter is a business that started in Richmond in 1876 and grew to be a national department store; there is still a Fenwicks in York. A replica 1950's post office shop was been built in the museum in 2007 and new interactive facilities opened in 2013.
- The Georgian Theatre Royal, founded in 1788 by the actor Samuel Butler, is just off the market place. A decline in the fortunes of theatre led to its closure in 1848 and it was used as a warehouse for many years. In 1963 the theatre was restored and reopened, with a theatre museum added in 1979. It was extended in 2003 with the addition of a new block providing services and access next to the original auditorium. It is the oldest working Georgian Theatre in UK which has seen many famous actors perform on its stage.
- The Station, a community-based social enterprise was formerly Richmond railway station. With a restaurant, 2-screen cinema, art gallery and heritage centre, as well as a bakery, cheese-maker, micro brewery, ice-cream parlour and fudge house, it averages 300,000 visitors a year

and is the fourth largest tourist attraction in Yorkshire. In 2008, it won the National Rail Heritage, Ian Allan Publishing award.

The Georgian Theatre Royal.

Richmond station.

Education

There are two secondary schools in the town. Richmond School and Sixth Form, which was extended 2012 at cost of £30m, has specialisms in Performing Arts, Science and Maths. There's also St Francis Xavier, a smaller comprehensive for boys and girls aged 11–16. Richmond has three primary schools: Richmond Methodist, Richmond C of E and St Mary's Roman Catholic School.

Panorama of Richmond falls, close to the town centre.

Richmond folk club.

Economy

Tourism is important to the local economy generating 75% of revenue, but the single largest influence is Catterick Garrison Army Base. This is rapidly becoming the largest population centre in Richmondshire and will be largest military base in the world for Great Britain when troops coming back from Germany in 2016.

Richmond cricket. Richmond, Yorkshire, at home, won this one.

Richmond cricket club v Shepherds Bush in London.
The Yorkshire team won by one run.

Richmond council meeting.

At the Great River Race. Left to right: Barclay Simpson, Deputy Mayor, Mayor Rita Palmer, Sheila, Mayor's consort.

Richmond Duck race May 6 2013. Buy a duck - all monies for a childrens charity.
Winner is the fastest duck to the lower bridge.

Richmond castle from the bridge where the ducks go in.

Richmond Yorkshire MP

The constituency presents itself as a safe seat for the Conservative Party, having held it continuously since 1910 (if including the 11 years by the allied Unionist Party from 1918). In the 2010 general election, Richmond produced the largest numerical and percentage majority for a Conservative, 62.8% of the vote.

The current MP, William Hague, has held the seat since a by-election in 1989 and has held the posts of Leader of the Opposition (1997–2001) and Foreign Secretary (2010–).

The constituency consists of in the west the entire Richmondshire district and in the east the northern part of Hambleton District. A mostly rural seat, the population is almost wholly self-supportive and in national terms affluent. Leyburn has a monthly farmers' market and the touristic traditional Wensleydale Railway was the scene for the 1960s-set long-running drama Heartbeat. Richmond town lost its own MP in 1885 and went to one MP.

History says Richmond was one of the parliamentary boroughs in the Unreformed House of Commons that dates to the middle of its long existence, first being represented in 1585. In modern times it has been an ultra-safe seat for the Conservative Party.

From 1983, the seat was represented by the cabinet minister Leon Brittan, after boundary changes saw his Cleveland and Whitby seat abolished; however he resigned from the Commons in December 1988 in order to take up the position of Vice-President of the European Commission.

William Hague is a very popular local MP and even in his very important role as Foreign Secretary he still makes time for all sorts of events in the constituency.

William Hague MP.

Mayor and Mayoress of Richmond N. Yorks Cllr Bob and Moira White

Bob and Moira settled in Richmond on his retirement from the army in 1988, having served 25 years with the Royal Corps of Signals. He went on to serve 16 years with the Yorkshire Ambulance Service as a Training Officer.

Having been elected to council in 2008 and now fully retired, Bob and Moira are able to dedicate their time to the duties of the Mayor of Richmond, which he feels is a great honour to be the first citizen of such an historic town. Bob and Moira are also active members of the Royal British Legion, Bob being the chairman of the local branch. He and Moira have produced and directed three Festivals of Remembrance in the town.

During his tenure Bob hopes to encourage greater co-operation between the various groups within the town to provide more facilities and events throughout the year.

Mayor & Mayoress of Richmond N.Yorks Cllr Bob and Moira White
2013 - 2014. Bob is the 345th Mayor.

"The Lass of Richmond Hill"

The song is a ballad of praise of and an expression of love for the "lass". It is widely thought to refer to Frances I'Anson, who the writer of the song, Irishman Leonard McNally married in 1787. Her family owned property called Hill House in Richmond, Yorkshire. George III said the song was a favourite of his.

It contains two verses with eight lines each and a chorus of four lines repeated after each verse. The first verse begins with the notable lines:

> *On Richmond Hill there lives a lass,*
> *More bright than May-day morn,*
> *Whose charms all other maids' surpass,*
> *A rose without a thorn.*
> The chorus:
> *Sweet lass of Richmond Hill,*
> *Sweet lass of Richmond Hill,*
> *I'd crowns resign to call thee mine,*
> *Sweet lass of Richmond Hill.*

According to the musicologist and conductor Peter Holman, *"a way of celebrating national identity was to place a love-story in a picturesque British rural setting. The most famous song of this type is James Hook's The Lass of Richmond Hill." (Source: Wikipedia)*

The song was seen as so quintessentially English that authorship by an Irishman, that is, by Leonard McNally, was periodically challenged and many other origins put forward though none of them have been proven.

The music was composed by James Hook (1746 – 1827), a composer and organist at Vauxhall Gardens from 1774 to 1820. Hook composed over 2,000 songs, the best known of which was "The Lass of Richmond Hill". It epitomises Hook's charming but sanitised folk-song style using a Scottish pastoral idiom, and is often mistakenly believed to be a genuine traditional folk song, and has been assigned the number 1246 on the Round Folk Song. Indeed, it has become a Scottish Folk Song. The song was first performed publicly by Charles Incledon at Vauxhall Gardens in 1789, although McNally appears to have written the words long before that. It became one of the most popular songs of the time and remains popular being played by the BBC's classical music station, Radio 3. As well as becoming a Scottish country dance, the music has been used as a military march by the British Army and is the regimental March of the Women's Royal Army Corps and the Middlesex Yeomanry. It was also the march of the 107 The Regiment of Foot Bengal Light infantry, a predecessor of the Royal Sussex Regiment.

The song, or its title, has been the subject of a wide variety of cultural references and allusions:

- The romantic metaphor "A rose without a thorn" was popularized by the song. It was subsequently much used: a recent example being by the singer-songwriter Nick Drake in his song "Time has told me."

- An early work by an Austrian composer entitled "The Lass of Richmond Hill" (Opus No. 2), is a variation for the piano and was published in 1791.
- *Sweet Lass of Richmond Hill* was the title of a 1970 historical novel about Mrs Fitzherbert by Eleanor Hibbert under the pen name "Jean Plaidy".
- A 1957 BBC film, directed by Rudolph Cartier, about Mrs Fitzherbert was called *The Lass of Richmond Hill.*
- *The Lass of Richmond Hill* was an 1877 painting by George Dunlop Leslie.
- According to a popular story, Richmond Hill Ontario gained its name from the nostalgic insistence of the town's first school teacher (from Richmond in England) that it should be named after the song.
- "Lass of Richmond Hill" is a pub in Richmond in London, the naming of which reflects earlier confusion between which of the two Richmonds the song concerned.

There is a pub for every day of the year, and a church for every Sunday.
(City of Norwich, 1939)
A village that loses its pub starts to die.
(John Adnams, Chairman, Adnams Brewery)
When you have lost your inns, drown you empty selves, for you will have lost the last of England. (Hilaire Belloc)

Lass of Richmond Hill pub in Richmond in London.

The Richmond Drummer Boy Legend

The legend maintains that many years ago, possibly at the end of the 18th century, some soldiers discovered an opening to a tunnel under the Keep of the Castle. As they were too large to crawl into it themselves, they selected one of the small regimental drummer boys to be lowered through a narrow crevice into a vault. He was told to continue along the passage beating his drum as he went. Guided by the sound of drumming, the soldiers were to follow his course above the ground and so plot the route.

The sound of the drum was heard clearly as he proceeded down the tunnel. It led them away from the Castle, across the Market Place in the direction of Frenchgate, and beside the River Swale towards Easby.

When the soldiers reached Easby Wood, half a mile from the Abbey, the drumming ceased. A stone stands today to mark the spot and is called the 'Drummer Boy Stone' by the local people. The drummer boy was never seen again. Perhaps the roof had fallen in? The mystery has never been solved.

Richmond Drummer Boy Walk

The Market Place is the starting point for this three mile (5km) circular walk past St Mary's Church and the Drummer Boy Stone, along the banks of the River Swale to Easby Abbey. The return route follows the old railway track to Richmond Castle.

Walk down across the cobblestones to the north east corner of the Market Place to a street leading north called Frenchgate. Turn north down Frenchgate past Swale House and right along Station Road past what was Richmond Lower School (will be the Council Offices in 2013). St Mary's Church is across the road on your left.

Walk down Station Road to the far end of the churchyard and turn left down a narrow lane called Lombards' Wynd. After about 30 metres you will reach a turning right along a path, sometimes known as Easby Low Road. On your left down the path you will see a green sign indicating 'Easby Abbey - 3/4 mile'.

Easby Low Road is the path to Easby Abbey along the bank of the River Swale. It leads upwards through Easby Wood with the fast flowing river down on the right. At the end of the wood, where a track leads down to the river, there is a gateway leading into a wide field. The Drummer Boy Stone - marking the spot where the soldiers last heard the sound of drumming - is mounted on a plinth.

Continue past the Drummer Boy Stone alongside the field on your left OR take the lower path with the river on your right and wooden fence on your left. Both paths come together at a stile. Continue by walking diagonally across the field towards the old Vicarage. Cross two more stiles and follow the path until you reach a metalled road.

Turn right down the lane, and on your left is the Gatehouse of the abbey, entered by a small gate in the iron fence. The Gatehouse is almost complete except for its roof, and still retains medieval vaulting. Continue a short distance down the lane to Easby Church.

From the church, walk towards a gravel path which leads along the bank of the River Swale. Easby Abbey is on your right. It is maintained by English Heritage and visitors are welcome to look around the ruins.

It is believed that the legendary tunnel was constructed in medieval times as an escape-route to the castle for the abbot and canons in case of attack from Scots, who frequently made raids into the northern counties.

Retrace your steps to the Car Park and head east along a gravel path alongside the River Swale. After about 300 metres, turn right across the old iron bridge and travel north along the old railway track towards Richmond.

Continue for about 1000 metres northward along the old railway track past the former railway station onto the A6136 road. Turn right and cross Station Bridge over the River Swale. Take the first gateway on the left which leads onto a path by the side of the river. The path leads onto Park Wynd and so to Millgate.

Turn north and climb up Millgate until you reach some steps on your left which rise up to Tower Street. From here you can see the Castle. *(By kind permission of richmod.org)*

The Ancient Silver Arrow

Once described as 'The Daddy of all Sporting Fixtures'; The Antient Silver Arrow, is the World's longest established and oldest recorded sporting event, dating back to 1673 and first shot for in Scorton Village Richmond, North Yorkshire.

The Society of Archers was formed at the first meeting of the Antient Silver Arrow Competition, to maintain Target Archery, the skill of which was largely in decline following the English Civil War.

The competition has continued annually since 1673 (except in periods of various Wars) and celebrated its tri-centenary shoot in 2008 with guest of honour The Rt Honourable William Hague MP.

The competition is open to any Gentleman Archer aged over 21 shooting in the Long Bow or any other bare bow and, since 1947, the Recurve Bow which was allowed to enter due to timber shortage and rationing in the UK following the war. Modern Compound bows are not permitted to take part.

The winner is the first gentleman to hit the 3 inch centre Black Spot (introduced in 1951 and first hit by Frank Newbould, Captain 1951 - previously it was just the Gold) at 100 yards and becomes 'Captain of the Arrow' and takes on the responsibility to arrange the next years meeting. Assisted by a Lieutenant, which is awarded to the first gentleman to hit the Red.

Entry in to the Competition automatically bestows the privilege to become a Member of the Society of Archers and to dine with the Captain and other members at the annual Luncheon. A blazer or jacket and tie must be worn during the luncheon and the AGM that follows (a Society Tie is available for purchase on the day).

It is fair to say that many gentleman archers attend 'the Scorton' for the sense of the occasion - an experience that has seen some members attending continually for over 60 years and others travelling from as far afield as the America's and Australia (countries even younger than our competition!) to renew the bond of friendship and sport between gentlemen at this most antient and unique event.

It is one of the few sporting fixtures where the competitor is at his own honour to mark his own score card, to be able to enjoy and share a drink on the field of play but where or unseemly behavior, such as cursing* would result in an immediate fine of up to one whole pound and the consternation of the judges who decision is final and without appeal. Proceeds of the 'swear bag' are given to a local charity incidentally.

(* Rumour has it that the Football Association are look are looking in to a similar rule for football players - though this is yet unconfirmed - or no it's not - see 'forum'!)

If this sounds like your kind of event - we would be delighted to welcome you to World's longest established and oldest recorded sporting event - The Antient Silver Arrow.

The 2013 Tournament will be the 305th Recorded Meeting in the 341st year of The Society of Archers and is to be held on Saturday 18th May 2013

Richmond, Yorkshire Septennial Boundary Riding

Among the many customs of great interest in the Town of Richmond, the Septennial Boundary Riding is perhaps the one of greatest interest. This custom takes the form of a "perambulation" as the appearance of those who have afterwards been permitted to sign the Roll (as having completed the walk) testifies.

The custom goes back to the Royal Charter given to the town by Elizabeth I in 1576 and is also confirmed under the Charter of Charles II 1668 that the Mayor, as Lord of the Manor, accompanied by his Councillors, Officers and townspeople should beat the bound of the town every seven years. The date however now usually occurs on the last Wednesday of August to allow schoolchildren to take part during their summer holidays.

At around 8.30 am, a picturesque procession assembles at the Town Hall and process to the starting point at Green Bridge.

The Procession:

- The Pinder, carrying as Pioneer, the Axe for the removal of any obstruction to the progress of the Riding.
- The Banner Bearer, with the Town Banner. He is followed by an ATC cadet carrying the Freedom Sword presented to the Town by the RAF Regiment when they were given the Freedom of the Town
- Two Halberdiers carrying their halberds and wearing their cloaks.
- Two Macebearers carrying the Great Mace and the Restoration Mace.
- The Mayor carrying the Mayor's Silver Mace in civic robes, accompanied by the Town Clerk.

The length of the town boundary is approximately 15 miles. At some points along the route proclamations are made by the Bellman against the adjoining parishes and Lords of the Manor.

The proclamation:

Oyez Oyez Oyez. I do in the name of the Mayor, Aldermen and Burgesses of the Borough of Richmond, Lords of the Manor and Borough of Richmond in the County of York hereby proclaim and declare this to be the ancient and undoubted bounday of the said Manor and Borough against the Manors or Lordships of...

Hipswell/Hudswell

Easby

Aske

Hipswell/Hudswell

God Save the Queen and the Lords of the Manors.

At two points along the route the Mayor is carried on the back of the Waterwader to the centre of the River Swale as the boundary at these points runs along the centre of the river (it is not unusual for the Mayor to get wet occasionally!). Having proceeded along the boundary to Sandford House where an out building straddles the boundary, the Mayor in time honoured tradition casts a stone over the roof to donate the boundary runs through the building.

On arrival at Olliver Ducket refreshments are served and a short break taken and then on again to Deepdale, arriving early afternoon. Here at Deepdale lunch is served and after lunch, foot races are held with prize money donated by local organisations or individuals. A race for Councillors being one of the highlights.

With Kind permision from Richmond.org

During the walk at five points along the route the Mayor throws freshly minted new pennies to the children. At the completion of the walk the Town Clerk enters the names in the roll of all who completed the full distance of the boundary and who may if they wish receive a certificate signed by the Mayor to that effect. Any donation for the certificate goes to the Mayoral Charities.

Photos taken from the Boundary walk (Richmond.org)

Links: Richmond, Yorkshire and America

Kiplin Hall

The house was built sometime during 1622–1625 for **George Calvert,** Secretary of State to James 1 who later became first Lord Baltimore and **Founder of Maryland** in what is now part of the USA. Initially built as a hunting lodge it was a slightly rectangular building fashioned of red brick with blue-black diamond-shaped tiles for decoration. Kiplin had four towers, which unusually, were not placed at the corners of the structure, but at the centre of each of the four walls - the north and south towers containing staircases, whilst the east and west comprised part of the rooms in which they were contained.

In 1722, Charles Calvert found himself in financial difficulties and sold the Kiplin Estate to his mother's second husband (his stepfather), Christopher Crowe for £7000 (approximately £550,000 in modern currency). Although not a member of the nobility, Crowe had been British Consul in Livorno, Italy and enjoyed the lucrative contract for supplying the British naval fleet with wine and olive oil. Combined with his activities in collecting antiquities for the British aristocracy his wealth and power grew. Purchasing Kiplin Hall around a century after its construction, he found the house to lack comfort: the Calverts had never lived there. A 'Gothic' wing was added in the 1820s and redesigned in 1887 by W.E. Nesfield.

Following extensive renovation and refurbishment, the house is now furnished as a comfortable Victorian home with 17 rooms open to view. Crowded with an eclectic mix of previous owners' furniture, paintings, portraits and personalia, including many Arts and Crafts items, there are also numerous original paintings from the 16th – 19th centuries are works by Beuckelaer, Carlevarijs, Kauffman and Watts. *(http://www.kiplinhall.co.uk/)*

The property is now open to the public and represents an insight into almost four centuries of life in North Yorkshire and the families who have lived in Kiplin Hall. A permanent exhibition charts the founding of Maryland by George Calvert.

Historic records of Kiplin Hall and its families from the early 18th century to the 21st century are held at the North Yorkshire County Record Office in Northallerton and at Kiplin Hall.

Kiplin - Education Connections with USA

The University of Maryland, with funding from the state of Maryland, in 1986 opened the *University of Maryland Study Center at Kiplin Hall,* established a resource *"built out of what was originally a stable house and blacksmith's shop."* It is open for students in the School of Architecture, Planning and Preservation and has residential facility for 20 students.

Washington College in Maryland offers a three-week summer program in English Literature. Lectures are presented each morning and students participate in afternoon field excursions. Significant historic, literary, landscape, and architectural sites of interest are part of field excursions. Influential literary figures such as Wordsworth, Coleridge, Shelley and others found the area around Kiplin Hall inspiring to their works.

The University of South Carolina has a summer programme in England to *"Provide comparisons with U.S. theory and practice in archives administration, museum management, and historic preservation. It offers behind-the-scenes tours of museums and historic sites, as well as meetings with curators, archivists, administrators, and government officials to discuss the practice of public history in the UK."* This includes Kiplin Hall. *(By kind permission of Kiplin Hall)*

<u>Francis Nicholson</u> (12 November 1655 – March 16, 1728)

Francis Nicholson was a British military officer and colonial administrator, born in Downholme, Richmond, Yorkshire. His military service included time in Africa and Europe, after which he was sent as leader of the troops supporting Sir Edmund Andros in the Dominion of New England. There he distinguished himself and was appointed lieutenant governor of the dominion in

1688. After news of the Glorious revolution reached the colonies in 1689, Andros was overthrown in the Boston Revolt. Nicholson himself was soon caught up in unrest in New York, and fled to England.

Francis next served as lieutenant governor or governor of Virginia and Maryland where he supported the founding of the College of William and Mary; however, he quarreled with Andros after Andros was selected over him as governor of Virginia. In 1709 he became involved in colonial military actions during Queen Anne's War, leading an aborted expedition against Canada. He then led the expedition that successfully captured Port Royal Acadia on 2 October 1710. Afterward he served as Governor of Nova Scotia and Placentia, and was the first royal governor of South Carolina following a rebellion against its proprietors. He rose to the rank of Lieutenant-General, and died a bachelor in London in 1728.

(Source: Susan A. Riggs, Manuscripts and Rare Books Librarian, Special Collections Research Center, Earl Gregg Swem Library College of William and Mary, P. O. Box 8794, Williamsburg, VA 23187-8794)

Pennsylvania, Maryland   Mason - Dixon Line

Jeremiah Dixon (July 27, 1733 – January 22, 1779) was an English surveyor and astronomer who is perhaps best known for his work with Charles Mason, from 1763 to 1767, in determining what was later called the Mason Dixon Line.

Dixon was born in Cockfield, near Bishop Auckland county Durham, in 1733, the fifth of seven children, to George Dixon and Mary Hunter. His father was a wealthy Quaker coalmine owner. Dixon became interested in astronomy and mathematics during his education at Barnard Castle and he worked at nearby Raby Estate as Surveyor.

Dixon and Mason signed an agreement in 1763 with the proprietors of Pennsylvania and Maryland Thomas Penn and Frederick Calvert, Sixth Baron of Baltimore, to assist with resolving a boundary dispute between the two provinces. They arrived in Philadelphia in November 1763 and began work towards the end of the year. The survey was not complete until late 1766 having covered 244 miles and stone markers every mile were imported from England Following his return to England in 1779, Dixon resumed his work as a surveyor at Raby Castle in Durham which is about 25 mins from Richmond. He died unmarried in Cockfield, January 22, 1779. There is exhibition in Bowes Museum Barnard Castle April – Oct 2013 on the Mason Dixon Line.

RICHMOND UPON THAMES

(Information and pictures reproduced with Kind permission from Angela Ivey Head of Tourism)

Welcome to London's most attractive borough, which for hundreds of years has been a favourite retreat of Royalty, the rich and the famous. Richmond lies 15 miles southwest of central London yet a fast train from London Waterloo will bring you here in 15 minutes.

When you arrive you will be in a different world. The River Thames runs through the heart of the borough for 21 miles linking Hampton Court Palace, Richmond town centre and Kew Gardens with central London. With beautiful Royal parks and historic houses, theatres, museums and galleries rich with exhibits and town centres bursting with shops and restaurants, Richmond upon Thames rivals anywhere in London.

The London Borough of Richmond upon Thames is a prosperous, safe and healthy borough. It covers an area of 5,095 hectares (14,591 acres) in Southwest London and is the only London borough spanning both sides of the Thames, with river frontage of 21½ miles. The main town centre is Richmond and there are four district centres at Twickenham, Teddington, East Sheen and Whitton.

Hundreds of years of royal history are still alive in Richmond. There are many magnificent historic buildings in and around the borough to choose from and be taken back in time to the Tudor, Stuart or Georgian times.

A 20-minute walk along the river from Richmond town Centre will take you to Ham House and Garden, an atmospheric Stuart mansion from 1610. The house remains a treasure trove of rare and unusual objects, with spectacular interiors and faithfully restored formal gardens. On the opposite bank of the Thames, attractively connected by Hammerton's passenger ferry, lies Marble Hill House, an elegant Palladian villa built in the 1720s for Henrietta Howard, the beloved mistress of King George II.

The world-famous Hampton Court Palace, surrounded by its amazing gardens on the banks of the River Thames, was the residence of Henry VIII, William III, Mary II and other royals from around 1500 to the first half of the 18ᵗʰ century. A day at the palace will take you through imaginative visitor routes to showcase exquisite tapestries, paintings, carvings and fully restored Tudor kitchens with live cookery taking place on selected days. Royal robes are available to wear to those wanting to experience what it might have felt like to be Henry VIII's Court!

Kew Gardens, the world's first and greatest botanic gardens, originated in the late 17ᵗʰ century. Princess Augusta and Lord Bute established the site as the first botanic gardens in 1759. Their remarkable horticultural and scientific history, royal heritage and historical importance led to recognition as UNESCO World Heritage Suite in 2003. Kew Palace, the earliest surviving building inside the Gardens was once home to King George III, Augusta's son, known as the 'mad King' due to a rare blood disorder, porphyria, the symptoms of which were tragically taken for madness.

World-renowned Royal Parks, stunning stretches of riverside and extravagantly planned public parks and gardens combine to make Richmond upon Thames the greenest and most beautiful borough in London. In addition, it's the only London borough to span both banks of the Thames.

The jewel in the crown is majestic Richmond Park, with its gently rolling hills, ancient copses and herds of free-roaming red and fallow deer, a landscape which has changed little from the days of Charles 1. From selected vantage points within this largest of the Royal Parks it is possible to view St Paul's Cathedral, the London Eye and other iconic central London landmarks.

The borough boasts over 100 parks, commons and woodlands which attract 5 million visitors each year. Numerous children's play areas have recently been refurbished, and new initiatives such as open air 'FitPoints', fitness activity groups and guided heath walks have been introduced to encourage people to make full use of these wonderful free facilities. Several council run spaces have been awarded the prestigious national Green Flag Award and there is an ongoing policy of improvement and regeneration.

The Terrace Gardens and Richmond Park in Richmond, York House and Radnor Gardens in Twickenham, and Carlisle Park in Hampton are especially popular. Each area of the borough has a village green, where summer fairs are held, cricket matches are played and families enjoy the rural peace and tranquility. Dotted throughout the borough you will discover pockets of greenery suitable for various outdoor activities including cycling, walking, picnicking and other outdoor pursuits. Visitors can discover rare trees, and many different types of flora and fauna in both formal and more rustic settings.

England's longest river, the Thames, is famous throughout the world for its history, its culture and its amazing variety of wildlife, archaeology and scenery. Richmond upon Thames without doubt boasts the most beautiful stretch of riverside in London. Together with the historic Richmond Bridge, which is an English Heritage Grade 1 listed structure, Petersham Meadows and Terrace Gardens, it is especially beautiful in Richmond itself. The view of the Thames from the top of Richmond Hill, protected by an Act of Parliament since 1902, has been a source of inspiration for artists and poets throughout the years.

Teddington Lock marks the boundary between the tidal and non-tidal Thames, and is a popular resting point for walkers on this stretch of the Thames Path. Running alongside or close to the River, this National Trail takes you through busy towns brimming with restaurants, cafes and pubs, and past wild commons and woodland where you may escape the bustle of city life. Islands dot the river, some forming residential hubs with houseboat moorings, boatyards and many different styles of accommodation, others are simply home to the vast assortment of wildfowl and animals that choose to live near the River.

Out on the water, passenger boats cruise upstream to Hampton Court or down to central London, offering an alternative and unique method of transport and an opportunity to discover the Thames from an entirely new perspective. If you are feeling energetic you can even hire a traditional Thames skiff or rowing boat and be captain for an hour, or a day! The river hosts many local events, ranging from regattas to dragon boat racing, and of course not forgetting the annual Oxford and Cambridge Boat Race and the annual Great River Race, held every year in September, which lays claim to being the longest river race in Europe.

The River has a special magic in Richmond upon Thames, offering an opportunity to spend tranquil hours exploring its banks on foot or by bike, which can also be hired from one of the boathouses near Richmond Bridge.

The London Borough of Richmond's is hosting the Gardens' Festival, which is a celebration of its gardens, past, present and future. It will explore the development of the English landscape garden through its exhibition Arcadian Vistas: Richmond's Landscape Gardens, which runs from 4 May – 21 July 2013 and showcases works from the Richmond Borough Art collection.

Leading the 1,000-strong flotilla to Queens Jubilee in 2012 was the Gloriana. The 94ft Royal rowbarge – the first to be built for more than a century – is unique among the participating vessels in that it is the only one specially commissioned for the event and was built by Richmond Boat

Builders owned by Mark Edwards and the Gloriana will be moored in Richmond upon Thames and used for special events.

Richmond upon Thames has over 160 local parks and gardens, many miles of towpath, Royal Parks and more than 40 play areas. It welcomes over 4.5 million visitors a year and the visitor economy is worth about £469 million.

In april 13 /14 2013 Richmond Yorkshire travelled to Richmond london for two games rained off. Yorkshire won the next game by one run

HRH Gloriana at Queen's Jubilee 2012. Photo courtesy eventphotography.co.uk

River race 2012. Photo courtesy eventphotography.co.uk

The two teams. Richmond Yorkshire above, Richmond London below. At the London ground.

Richmond cricket. London v Yorkshire Sept 15 2012

Richmond Theatre

Adjacent to Richmond Green, it opened on 18 September 1899 with a performance of *As You Like It* and is one of the finest surviving examples of the work of theatre architect Frank Macham. John Earl, writing in 1982, described it as: *"Of outstanding importance as the most completely preserved Matcham Theatre in Greater London and one of his most satisfying interiors."* The theatre, originally known as the *Richmond Theatre and Opera House*, is structured into the familiar stalls, dress and upper circles, with four boxes at dress level. The auditorium is a mixture of gilt detailing and red plush fabrics, covering seats and front of circles.

In the early 1990s the theatre underwent a major overhaul overseen by the designer Carl Toms. This included a side extension giving more space for the audience and includes a 'Matcham Room in Theatre and theatre is sited adjacent to Little Green. Its interior and exterior has been used as a movie set in many films (e.g. Evita, Finding Neverland and doubling as the Dukes of York Theatre - setting of Ford's Theatre) and TV programmes (e.g. Jonathan Creek). The theatre has a weekly schedule of plays and musicals, usually given by professional touring companies. Pre-West End shows can sometimes be seen. There is a Christmas and New Year pantomime tradition and many of Britain's greatest music hall and pantomime performers have appeared there.

Orange Tree Theatre

As a company the First Orange Tree Theatre, then known as the Richmond Fringe, was founded on 31 December 1971 by its present artistic director, Sam Walters and his actress wife Auriol Smith, in a small room above the Orange Tree pub, close to Richmond railway station. Six former church pews, arranged around the performing area, were used to seat an audience of up to 80 in number. Initially productions were staged in daylight and at lunchtimes. But when theatre lighting and window-blinds were installed, matinee and evening performances of full-length plays also became possible. The London critics regularly reviewed its productions and the venue gained a reputation for quality and innovation, with theatre-goers queuing on the stairs, waiting to purchase tickets.

The New Orange Tree Theatre

As audience numbers increased there was pressure to find a more accommodating space, both front and backstage. On 14 February 1991, the company opened its first production across the road in the current premises, the new Orange Tree Theatre housed within a converted primary school. Meanwhile the original theatre continued to function as a second stage for shorter runs and works in translation until 1997 and renamed The Room (above the pub). Design of both the school conversion and construction were undertaken by Iain Macintosh as head of the Theatre Projects Consultants team. The design intent was to retain the same sense of intimacy as the old theatre, thus calling for an unusually small acting area.

The solution was to create, at stage level, no more than three rows of shallow raked seating on any side of the acting area, plus an irregular, timber-clad gallery above of only one row (which helps to 'paper the wall with people') under which actors could circulate on two sides to reach the stage entrances at all four corners of the playing space. Foyers and dressing rooms were sited in the rebuilt house of the former headmaster, while the theatre space itself is built where once were the assembly hall and school playground.

Any fears that the special atmosphere of the old theatre would be lost have proved totally unfounded, and close links have been formed with the Stephen Joseph Theatre in Scarborough, also founded as an in-the-round theatre by Sir Alan Ayckbourn.

Costs of development

The total construction and conversion cost including shell. Fitting out, fees etc., was estimated at £1,750,000. The developers County and District Properties and Grosvenor Developments provided the shell structure, worth £1,000,000, as a "planning gain" for a development which also includes the European headquarters of Pepsi-Cola International. This left £750,000 to be raised by a Theatre Appeal, launched in 1988 by Richmond residents Sir Richard and Lady Attenborough.

2003 extension

In 2003 the former Royal Bank of Scotland building next door to the new theatre was modified and re-opened as a dedicated space for rehearsals, set-building and costume storage, significantly expanding and improving its operation

Hampton Court Palace

The world-famous Hampton Court Palace, surrounded by its amazing gardens on the banks of the River Thames, was the residence of Henry VIII, William III and Mary II and other royals from around 1500 o the first half of 18th century. A day at the palace will take you through imaginative visitor routes to showcase exquisite tapestries, paintings, carvings and fully restored Tudor kitchens with live cookery taking place on selected days. Royal robes are available to wear to those wanting to experience what might have felt like to be at Henry VIII's Court!

Hampton Court Palace.

Kew Gardens

Kew Gardens, the world's first and greatest botanic gardens, originated in the late 17th century. Princess Augusta and Lord Bute established the site as the first botanic gardens in 1759. Their remarkable horticultural and scientific history, royal heritage and historical importance led to recognition as a UNESCO World Heritage Site in 2003. Kew Palace, the earliest surviving building inside the Gardens, was once home to King George III, Augusta's son, known as the 'mad King' due to a rare blood disorder, porphyria, the symptoms of which were tragically taken for madness.

Richmond Palace

This was a royal residence on the right (south, or Surrey) bank of the river Thames, upstream of the Palace of Westminster, to which it lay 9 miles (14 km) SW of as the crow flies. It was erected c. 1501 within the royal manor of Sheen by Henry VII, formerly known by his title Earl of Richmond after which it was named from Richmond Yorkshire. It was occupied by royalty until 1649.

It replaced a former palace, itself built on the site of a manor house that had been appropriated by the Crown some two centuries beforehand, which had been in royal possession for most of that time.

In 1500, immediately preceding the construction of the new "Richmond" Palace the following year, the town of Sheen which had grown up around the royal manor changed its name to "Richmond", by command of Henry VII. The two separate nomenclatures of *Sheen* and *Richmond* continue to this day, not without scope for confusion, since today's districts called "East Sheen" and "North Sheen", now under the administrative control of the London Borough of Richmond. Richmond remained part of the County of Surrey until the mid-1960s, when it was absorbed by the expansion of London.

Of Richmond Palace today only vestigial traces remain, most notably the Gatehouse. The site occupies the area between Richmond Green and the River Thames, the street names of which provide evidence of the former existence of the Palace, namely Old Palace Lane, Old Palace Yard and The Wardrobe.

Norman History of the Palace

HENRY I lived briefly in the King's house in Sheen spelt anciently, Shene.

In 1299 Edward 1 took his whole court to the manor-house at Sheen, close by the river side, which thus became a *Royal Palace*. William Wallace was executed in London in 1305, and it was in Sheen that the Commissioners from Scotland went down on their knees before Edward. When the boy-king Edward III came to the throne in 1327 he gave the manor to his mother Isabella. Almost 50 years later, after his wife Philippa died, Edward spent over 2,000 pounds on improvements. In the middle of the work Edward III himself died at the manor in 1377. In 1368 Geoffrey Chaucer served as a Yeoman at Sheen.

RICHARD II was the first English king to make Sheen his main residence in 1383. He took his bride Anne of Bohemia there. Twelve years later Richard was so distraught at the death of Anne at the age of 28, that he, according to Holinshed *"caused it [the manor] to be thrown down and defaced; whereas the former kings of this land, being wearie of the citie, used customarily thither to resort as to a place of pleasure, and serving highly to their recreation."* For almost 20 years it lay in ruins until Henry V undertook rebuilding work in 1414. The first, pre-Tudor, version of the palace was known as Sheen Palace. It was positioned roughly in what is now the garden of Trumpeters' House, between Richmond Green and the River. In 1414 Henry V also founded a Carthusian monastery there known as Sheen Priory, adjacent on the North to the Royal residence.

Henry VII, Builder of Richmond Palace

In 1492 a great tournament was held at the Palace by Henry VII. On 23 December 1497 a fire destroyed most of the wooden buildings. Henry rebuilt it and named the new palace "Richmond" Palace after his title of Earl of Richmond as his Earldom was seated at Richmond Castle Yorkshire, from which it took its name. In 1502, the new palace witnessed a betrothal. Princess Margaret, daughter of Henry VII, became engaged to King James IV. From this line eventually came the House of Stuart. In 1509 Henry VII died at Richmond Palace.

Henry VIII

Later the same year, Henry VIII celebrated Christmas to Twelfth Night at Richmond with the first of his six wives, Catherine of Aragon. During those celebrations, says Mrs A .T Thomson, in her *Memoirs of the Court of Henry the Eighth*:

"In 1533 Richmond became the principal residence of Henry's daughter after she was evicted from her previous residence of Beaulieu. Mary stayed at the palace until December of that year when she was ordered to Hatfield House to wait on the newly born Princess Elizabeth."

(Over the next hundred years from 1509, the Christmas celebrations gradually increased with music, dancing, theatricals and revels. The 12 days of Christmas were barely celebrated before the sixteenth century. By the time Elizabeth 1 died at Richmond in 1603, celebrating Christmas was well established in court circles.)

Almost nothing survives of earlier manors. In the 1520s, Cardinal Wolsey adopted new renaissance architectural styles at Hampton Court Palace. This was only a few miles from Richmond and Henry was boiling with jealousy. On Wolsey's fall, he confiscated it and forced him to accept Richmond Palace in exchange. In his Chronicles, Hall says *"when the common people, and especially such as had been servants of Henry VII, saw the Cardinal keep house in the manor royal at Richmond, which that monarch so highly esteemed, it was a marvel to hear how they grudged, saying, 'so a butcher's dogge doth lie in the manor of Richmond!'"*.

In 1540 Henry gave the palace to his fourth wife, Anne of Cleves, as part of her divorce settlement.

Mary I

In 1554 Queen Mary married Phillip II of Spain. Forty-five years after her mother Catherine of Aragon had spent Christmas at Richmond Palace, they spent their honeymoon there and at Hampton Court. Later that same year, the future Elizabeth I was held prisoner at Richmond by Mary I. Mary's father Henry VIII married Anne Boleyn and produced a daughter, Elizabeth. Despite periods of closeness throughout their childhood, Mary grew to fear her half-sister's claim to the throne and their relationship deteriorated. When Mary became queen she chose to banish her own half-sister to Richmond Palace.

Elizabeth I

Once Elizabeth became queen she spent much of her time at Richmond, as she enjoyed hunting stags in the "Newe Parke of Richmonde" (now the Old Deer Park). Elizabeth died there on 24 March 1603.

James I

King James I preferred the Palace of Westminster to Richmond. Like Elizabeth, James enjoyed hunting stags, and in 1637 created a new area for this now known as Richmond Park, renaming Elizabeth's "Newe Parke" the "Old Deer Park". There continue to be red deer in Richmond Park today, possibly descendants of the original herd, free from hunting and relatively tame.

Charles I and Commonwealth

Charles I before he became king owned Richmond Palace and started to build his art collection whilst living there.

Within months of the execution of Charles in 1649, Richmond Palace was surveyed by order of Parliament to see what it could fetch in terms of raw materials, and was sold for £13,000. Over the next ten years it was largely demolished, the stones being re-used as building materials.

Surviving structures

- These include the Wardrobe, Trumpeters' House and the Gate House. The latter was built in 1501, and was let on a 65-year lease by the Crown Estate Commissioners in 1986. It has five bedrooms.
- During 1997 the site was investigated in the Channel 4 programme 'Time Team', which was broadcast in January 1998. In summer, Trumpeters House is used for garden parties.
- This palace was one of the first buildings in history to be equipped with a flushing lavatory, invented by Elizabeth I's godson, Sir John Harringdon. Henry VIII had earlier installed flushing latrines at Hampton Court.

The current Mayor of Richmond upon Thames (2012-2013) is Rita Palmer.

Richmond Hill in London is a hill that rises gently on its northern side from the ancient Thames meadow-lands around the site of Richmond Palace up to and slightly beyond the Richmond Gate entrance to Richmond Park, the former royal hunting grounds enclosed by Charles 1. The descent south-westwards from this point back down to the upstream meadows is noticeably steeper, although the down gradient is less marked on its southerly and easterly progress through the park itself.

This renowned hill offers the only view in England to be protected by an Act of Parliament - the Richmond, Ham and Petersham Open Spaces Act passed in 1902 - to protect the land on and below Richmond Hill and thus preserve the fine foreground views to the west and south. Immortalised in paintings by Sir Joshua Reynolds and JMW Turner, it was described by Sir Walter Scott as "an unrivalled landscape".

The scenic panorama may be viewed from Terrace Walk, laid out near the top of the hill in the 18th century. This promenade surmounts the Terrace Gardens and both are Grade 11. As the town of Richmond developed from its founding in the early 16th Century, after Henry VII had established Richmond Palace, the attributes of the hill naturally attracted desirable residential and commercial development - with the result that many substantial properties came and went on the hill over the centuries, some of them with famous or notable persons as owners or occupiers. That situation is still in vogue today.

The original homes on Richmond Hill were built in what is now The Vineyard, including Vineyard House, Clarence House, Michel's Almshouses and Halford House. Clarence House was built in the 1690s for Nathaniel Rawlins, a London haberdasher merchant, who lived there until his death in 1718. The Duke of Clarence, future King William IV lived in Richmond in the late 1780s and gave his name to the property. From 1792 to 1799, Clarence House was a Catholic school run by Timothy Eeles. Among the students was Bernardo O'Higgins, the future independence leader of Chile.

Links with America

The Smithsonian Institute, Washington

British scientist and mineralogist, **James Smithson** (ca. 1765 – 27 June 1829) left most of his wealth to a nephew, but when the nephew died childless in 1835, under Smithson's will the estate passed *"to the United States of America, to found at Washington, under the name of the Smithsonian Institution, an Establishment for the increase & diffusion of knowledge among men."*

Smithson was the illegitimate child of the 1st Duke of Northumberland, and was born James Lewis Macie, in secret in Paris. Eventually he was naturalized in England and he attended college, studying chemistry and mineralogy.

The **Smithsonian Institution** established in *1846 "for the increase and diffusion of knowledge"*, is a group of museums and research centres administered by the United States government. Termed *"the nation's attic" which some people call the Smithsonian* for its eclectic holdings of 137 million items, the Institution's Washington, D.C. nucleus of nineteen museums, nine research centres, and zoo—many of them historical or architectural landmarks—is the largest such complex in the world. Additional facilities are located in Arizona, Maryland, New York City, Virginia, Panama and elsewhere, and 168 other museums are Smithsonian affiliates. The Institution's thirty million annual visitors are admitted without charge; funding comes from the Institution's own endowment, private and corporate contributions, membership dues, government support, and retail, concession and licensing revenues. Institution publications include Smithsonian magazines.

The current Duke of Northumberland owns Syon Park in Richmond upon Thames which has been in family ownership for 400 years. Henry VIII was laid to rest at Syon Park and his coffin came open during night. *(By kind permission of visitrichmond.co.uk)*

Richmond, The American International University in London

This is a private, liberal arts and professional studies University, internationally accredited and established in 1972 in Richmond, London. One of a number of American universities located outside the USA, its student body comes from over 90 countries, naturally including the USA, but also with growing numbers from the UK, who value the small class sizes, high contact hours and integral internships that sets Richmond apart from many UK Universities. Uniquely, its degrees are both accredited in the USA by the Middle States Commission on Higher Education and validated in the UK by the Open University Validation Services (OUVS).

Split between two campuses both in the Greater London area, the Richmond Campus is located near the crest of Richmond Hill, while the central London campus is located just off Kensington High Street. The Richmond Campus, a seat of higher learning since 1851, is the initial residence of most undergraduate students, especially freshman who have just enrolled at the university; its facade is a major symbol of the school and appears on almost all promotional literature. The school's headquarters and admissions department are also located here. Typical of city-centre universities, the Kensington Campus, by contrast, is a closely grouped set of buildings rather than a single site. It is where many of the upper-level undergraduate students reside, alongside the Masters programmes.

Prospective students and their families are always welcome to visit the University, either on an organised Open Day or by individual appointment. See www.richmond.ac.uk. Email enroll@richmond.ac.uk or telephone +44 (0) 208 332 9000.

The Development & Alumni Relations team exists to help Richmond alumni develop their links with and benefit from the University's global alumni community. We work with alumni volunteers to plan events and reunions and to establish local chapters around the world. We support alumni to stay in touch and up-to-date with each other and the University. Most of all, we work to involve alumni in the future of the University.

We are always pleased to hear from you:

Ms Karen Lippoldt, Director of Development & Alumni Relations
Development & Alumni Relations
Richmond, The American International University in London
Queen's Road, Richmond-upon-Thames
Surrey, TW10 6JP, UK
Email: alumni@richmond.ac.uk Telephone: +44 (0) 208 332 8341

Mayor, Cllr Meena Bond of Richmond London 2013 - 2014.

Present Member of Parliament for Richmond Park, Zac Goldsmith MP

I've been lucky enough to live in Richmond most of my life, which makes representing it in Parliament an enormous privilege. What makes this constituency special are the communities within it. Unlike so many urban areas, Richmond Borough is a network of unique villages, from Barnes and Kew to Sheen, Richmond itself and Ham. Richmond Park is London's jewel; a nature paradise on the edge of a heaving city. It is said that it has more ancient trees than all of France and Germany combined; an exaggeration no doubt, but an acceptable one! As if that's not enough, the Borough is home to Kew Gardens, a global monument to biodiversity and ecological expertise.

Zac Goldsmith
MP Richmond Park
APRIL 2013

For more information:
Web: wwwvisitrichmond.co.uk   Email: info@visitrichmond.co.uk
Facebook: Visit Richmond, Surrey   Twitter: @ Visit_ Richmond

RICHMONDS: USA

RICHMOND, VIRGINIA

Richmond is city in Virginia, which is a state in the South Region of the USA. It has a population of 200,000 and the adjacent counties of Henrico and Chesterfield combine to create a local population of more than 1,250,000 people.

Richmond has been called a city of neighbourhoods, each one with a distinct look, flavour, and identity. All are recognized by Richmonders as unique neighbourhoods, almost as though the city were a collection of several small towns.

Richmond is the capital of the Commonwealth of Virginia. It was settled in 1607 by English settlers named Captain Christopher Newport and Captain John Smith. The site was previously inhabited by the Powhatan Indians. It was named Richmond after the London suburb of Richmond-upon-Thames by its founder William Byrd II. The settlement did not become a city until 1742, and in the 135 years in-between served as little more than a trading post for furs, hides, and tobacco. In 1782 Richmond became the state capital of Virginia.

Richmond is one of the oldest American cities. The Shockoe Bottom entertainment area is where slave rebellion leader Gabriel had his head hung from a pike. During the American Civil War, it served as the capital of the Confederacy. When the Northern Army invaded Richmond, the fleeing Confederate government set fire to the city's munitions stores and government records they were unable to take with them. The fire grew out of control when winds picked up, and most of the city burned. The soldiers from the Union helped to put out the fires upon their arrival. The day after the city fell, Abraham Lincoln made a visit to the city.

Capitol Hill.

Richmond Attractions

Though much of its colonial past has disappeared, it is rich in Civil War history and lore. There are, among other things, a Civil War prison site on Belle Isle, the house Robert E. Lee lived in, the state Capitol (which Thomas Jefferson designed and said was inspired by the Maison Carrée at Nimes France), which served as the Confederate Capitol during the war, a museum of the Confederacy, the original Confederate White House, and Hollywood Cemetery in the heart of the city where more than 18,000 Confederate soldiers are laid to rest. Richmond has the most forged iron outside of New Orleans and one of the first African American neighbourhoods (Jackson Ward).

An island In the middle of the James River. It offers great views of the falls and the river, but be wary of copperheads, which abound on the island. A Copperhead was a member of a vocal group of Democrats was located in the Northern United States of the Union who opposed the American Civil War, wanting an immediate peace settlement with the Confederates. Republicans started calling antiwar Democrats "Copperheads", likening them to the Venomous snake. The Peace Democrats accepted the label, reinterpreting the copper "head" as the likeness of Liberty, which they cut from copper pennies and proudly wore as badges– Many teenagers enjoy swimming and laying out on the rocks and there are rope swings set up on the bridges nearby. It is a great hangout for teenagers and young adults.

American Civil War Museum.

Maymont Park

A wealthy landowner donated his estate to the city and Richmond turned it into one of the most beautiful urban parks in the nation. Fountains, Italianate gardens and a Japanese tea garden are a pleasure to walk through. The nature centre here is all-encompassing and free, and its exhibits on Virginia Wildlife include two otters that are glad to show off for visitors. Grey foxes, red-tailed hawks, and other exhibits are located outside. Children like the farm area where sheep, lambs, chickens, and other sundry animals are exhibited.

The Tredegar Iron Works, American Civil War Center, Richmond National Battlefield Headquarters at Tredegar, 490 Tredegar Street

The site of a Civil War era iron foundry which supplied ordinance to the Confederate Army. The site has long been the NPS headquarters and Museum of the Richmond/Petersburg Battlefield area and just recently ground was broken on the American Civil War Centre, which aims to be the definitive museum on interpretation of the conflagration from all perspectives. Also on the grounds are a statue of Abraham Lincoln and his son Todd.

Museum of the Confederacy, 1201 East Clay Street at 12th Street

The Museum is looking to expand into a state-wide system of museums, while maintaining its headquarters in Richmond. It contains the largest collection of Confederate records, artefacts and other treasures from the period. The Museum also maintains and gives tours of the White House of the Confederacy.

The White House of the Confederacy, East Clay and 12th Street

This has been restored to reflect its use as the executive mansion of Confederate President Jefferson Davis during the Civil War. Open to the public with regularly scheduled guided tours that are arranged and given by the Museum of the Confederacy.

Hollywood Cemetery, 412 South Cherry Street

Located between the neighbourhoods of Oregon Hill and Randolph on a bluff overlooking the

James River, Presidents Tyler and Monroe have their final resting places here. So does the locally renowned Jefferson Davis, and it's worth the trip through winding roads to see reverent Southerners laying flags on his grave. Also in the cemetery are Confederate Generals George Pickett and J.E.B. Stuart and local authors James Branch Cabell and Ellen Glasgow. The lines of small headstones marking the mass graves of Confederate dead is sobering and gratifying.

Lewis Ginter Botanical Garden.

Lewis Ginter Botanical Garden, 1800 Lakeside Avenue

An oasis of year-round beauty and interest, the Garden has more than a dozen themed areas including a Rose Garden, a Healing Garden, Asian Valley, Historic Bloemendaal House, a Victorian-style garden and a Children's Garden – complete with wheelchair accessible Tree House and Water Play. The glass Conservatory is the only one of its kind in the mid-Atlantic. The Garden Shop offers distinctive items; dining is available in the Garden Café and Tea House. Lewis Ginter Botanical Garden is a place to learn about plants, to marvel at nature, to relax, to take gardening classes, or to have a wedding or a business meeting. A wide variety of experiences are offered through its diverse gardens and facilities. Lewis Ginter Botanical Garden is consistently one of the most-visited attractions in the Richmond area.

The Garden is open daily from 9 a.m. to 5 p.m. The Garden is closed on Thanksgiving Day, Dec. 24 and Dec. 25.

Other interesting places

- Byrd Park: there are fishing lakes, seasonal paddle boats, a fitness trail and the Dogwood Dell amphitheatre home to the Summer Festival of Arts
- Virginia Fine Arts Museum, 200 North Boulevard
- Science Museum of Virginia, 2500 West Broad Street
- The Children's Museum of Richmond, 2626 W Broad Street
- Black History Museum
- Edgar Alan Poe Museum
- The Landmark Theatre (formerly The Mosque), 6 North Laurel Street

- Regularly features off-Broadway plays in addition to hosting comedians from around the nation
- State Capitol, Bank Street. The structure was designed by Thomas Jefferson and is the current home of the Virginia General Assembly. From 1861-1865 it also served as the home of the Confederate States Congress
- Egyptian Building, East Broad Street. This was the first building and home of the Medical College of Virginia, which now surrounds the structure
- Carytown. If you like to shop, the here is a must. The prices are high, but the high-end clothing, art, and antiques are worth it. Check out the restaurants while you're there - some of the best eateries in Richmond

Fine Arts Museum.

Chesterfield House.

Richmond Museum.

Music

Despite churning out a good number of internationally known rock, indie, metal, punk and R&B acts, many outsiders don't think of the former capital of the Confederacy as being a hotbed of diverse musical arts. However, largely thanks to the thriving arts scene associated with and around Virginia Commonwealth University, Richmond has a great music scene. Clubs offer a diverse selection of genres from rock, indie, metal, punk, hardcore, alternative, blues, jazz, jam, country and bluegrass. In addition to international and national acts that come through town, there is a vibrant (and often fiercely independent) local music scene which has spawned a good number of internationally renowned acts in recent years.

Work

The Greater Richmond area was named the third-best city for business by Market Watch in September 2007, ranking behind only the Minneapolis and Denver areas and just above Boston and even though date is little old Richmond is still thriving business city today. The area is home to six Fortune 500 companies, including: electric utility Dominion Resources; CarMax; Owens & Minor; Genworth Financial, the former insurance arm of GE; MeadWestvaco; and Altria Group. Only Dominion Resources and MeadWestvaco are headquartered within the city of Richmond; the others are located in the neighbouring counties of Henrico and Hanover. In 2008, Altria moved its corporate HQ from New York City to Richmond, adding another Fortune 500 corporation to Richmond's list. Five Fortune 1000 companies also have their headquarters located in the area. These include: Brink's; Massey Energy; Universal Corporation; and Markel. Of these, only Massey Energy and Universal Corporation are headquartered within the city limits. Other Fortune 500 companies, while not headquartered in the area, do have a major presence. These include SunTrust Bank (based in Atlanta), Capital One Financial Corporation (officially based in McLean, Virginia, but founded in Richmond with its operations centre and most employees in the Richmond area), and the medical and pharmaceutical giant McKesson (based in San Francisco). Capital One and Altria Company's Philip Morris USA are two of the largest private Richmond-area employers. DuPont maintains a production facility in South Richmond known as the Spruance Plant. *(Source: Wikipedia)*

Education

University of Richmond

This is a private non-sectarian liberal arts university located on the border of the city of Richmond and Henrico County Virginia. The University of Richmond is a primarily undergraduate, residential university with approximately 4,250 undergraduate and graduate students in five schools: the School of Arts and Sciences, the E Clabourne Robins School of Business, the Jepson School of Leadership Studies and the School of Law.

Dragon boat racing in Richmond, Virginia.

First Friday art walk.

RICHMOND COUNTY, VIRGINIA

This is a county located on the Northern Neck in the Commonwealth of Virginia, a state in the USA; the county seat is Warsaw. As of 2010, the population was 9,254. The rural county should not be confused with the large city and state capital Richmond, Virginia, which is over an hour's drive away. A notable attraction is the nationally protected area Rappahannock River Valley National Wildlife Refuge.

Here are adjoining counties named after places in the 'Old Country'.

Westmoreland County   - North
Northumberland County   - East
Lancaster County   - South-east
Essex County   - South-west

RICHMOND, ARIZONA

Richmond in Cochise County was a 'suburb' of Tombstone, itself now a ghost town and is located about 1 mile south of the Tombstone Courthouse. Only some foundations and adobe wall remnants remain.

RICHMOND, WESTERN CONTRA COSTA COUNTY, CALIFORNIA

The earliest inhabitants of Richmond were the Ohlone Indians, settling here an estimated 5,000 years ago. Distinct and separate groups of a few hundred individuals lived a stable and peaceful existence, with a culture based on strong community ties, spiritualism, and rich artistic creativity. The Ohlone were hunters and gatherers and built extensive shell-mounds along the Bay. With the coming of the Europeans the Ohlone way of life gradually came to an end and was destroyed.

The first Europeans to visit the city's future site were the Spanish explorers Pedro Fages and Reverend Juan Crespi who passed through the East Bay in 1772. After Mexico won independence from Spain in 1821, large tracts of land in California were granted to military heroes and loyalists. In 1823, Don Francisco Castro was given 17,000 acres of land in Contra Costa which became known as Rancho San Pablo. The city of Richmond was established on a portion of Castro's land grant about seventy years after his death.

The city was incorporated on August 7, 1905. Located in the Eastern region of the San Francisco, Richmond is the largest city in the United States served by the Green Party. As of the 2010 US Census the city's population is 103,701.

At the outset of World War II, four Richmond shipyards were built along the Richmond waterfront, employing thousands of workers, many recruited from all over the United States, including many African-Americans and women entering the workforce for the first time. Many of these workers lived in specially constructed houses scattered throughout the San Francisco Bay Area, including Richmond, Berkeley and Albany. A specially built rail line, the Shipyard Railway transported workers to the shipyards. Kaiser's Richmond shipyards built 747 Victory and Liberty Ships for the war effort, more than any other site in the U.S. The city broke many records and even built one Liberty ship in a record five days. On average the yards could build a ship in thirty days. The medical system established for the shipyard workers at the Richmond field Hospital eventually became today's Kaiser Permante HMO. It remained in operation until 1993 when it was replaced by the modern Richmond Medical Center hospital that has subsequently expanded to a large multiple building campus.

Point Richmond was originally the commercial hub of the city, but a new down-town arose in the centre of the city. It was populated by many department stores such as Kress, J C Penney, Sears, Macys, and Woolworths. During the war the population increased dramatically and peaked at around 120,000 by the end of the war. Once the war ended the shipyard workers were no longer needed, beginning a decades-long population decline. The Census listed 99,545 residents in 1950. By 1960 much of the temporary housing built for the shipyard workers was torn down, and the population dropped to about 71,000. Many of the people who moved to Richmond were black and came from the Midwest and South. Most of the white men were overseas at war, and this opened up new opportunities for ethnic minorities and women. This era also brought with it the innovation of day-care for children, as a few women could care for several dozen women's children, while most of the mothers went off to work in the factories and shipyards.

During World War II, Richmond developed rapidly as a heavy industrial town, chiefly devoted to shipbuilding. Its major activity now is as a seaport, with 26 million tons of goods shipped through Port Richmond in 1993, mostly oil and petroleum products. Chevron USA has a major oil refinery in the city, with a storage capacity of 15 million barrels (2,400 m^3). In the 1970s the Hilltop area including a large shopping mall was developed in the Northern suburbs of the city; this further depressed the down-town area as it drew away retail clients and tenants. In the late 1990s and early 2000s the Richmond Parkway was built along the Western industrial and North-western parkland of the city connecting Interstates 80 and 580.

In the early 1900s, the Santa Fe railroad established a major rail-yard adjacent to Point Richmond. The railroad constructed a tunnel through the Potrero San Pablo ridge to run a track from their yard to a ferry landing from which freight cars could be trans-shipped to San Francisco. Where this track crosses the main street in Point Richmond, there remain two of the last operational 'wigwag' crossing signals in the United States, and the only surviving examples of the "upside-down" type. The 'wigwag' is an antiquated type of railroad crossing signal which was phased out in the 1970s and 80s across the country. There was controversy in 2005 when the State Transportation Authority ordered the BNSF railroad company to upgrade the railroad crossing signals. A compromise was achieved that included installing new modern crossing gates, red lights and bells while not removing, but simply shutting off the historic ones and preserving their functionality for special events

The Pullman Company also established a major facility in Richmond in the early 20th century that connected with both the Santa Fe and Southern Pacific and serviced their passenger coach equipment. The Pullman Company was a large employer of African-American men, who worked mainly as porters on the Pullman cars. Many of them settled in the East Bay, from Richmond to Oakland, prior to World War II.

In 2006 the city celebrated its centennial. This coincided with the repaving and street paving project of McDonald Avenue. The city's old run-down commercial district along Macdonald has been designated the city's "Main Street District" by the state of California. This has led to funding of improvements in the form of state grants.

Other facts

- Until the enactment of prohibition in 1919, the city had the largest winery in the world; the small abandoned village of Wine Haven remains fenced off along Western Drive in the Point Molate area.
- Standard oil set up operations here in 1901, including what is now the Chevron Richmond Refinery which is still operated by Chevron. There is a pier into San Francisco Bay south of Point Molate for oil tankers.
- The Ku Klux Klan was active in the city in the 1920s.
- In 1930 the Ford Motor Company opened an assembly plant which moved to Milpitas in the 1960s. The old Ford plant has been a National Historic Place since 1988, and has recently been converted into an events centre (Ford Point Building – The Craneway).
- Until the onset of World War II it was a small town, but a rush of migrants in the 1940s caused a boom in the industrial sector.
- Martin Luther King JR had planned to visit Richmond just prior to his assassination.

RICHMOND DISTRICT, SAN FRANCISCO

Aerial view of Richmond District as of May 2012.

Originally an expanse of rolling sand dunes, the district was developed initially in the late 19th century. Adolph Sutro was one of the first large-scale developers of the area. After purchasing the Cliff House in the early 1880s, he built the Sutro Baths on the Western end of the district, near Ocean Beach.

After the 1906 earthquake development increased with the need to provide replacement housing. The last of the sand dunes and coastal scrub that once dominated the area were built over to create a street car suburb.

In the 1950s, and especially after the lifting of the Chinese Exclusion Act in 1965, Chinese immigrants began to replace the ethnic Jewish and Irish-Americans who had dominated the district before World War II. Chinese by birth or descent now make up nearly the majority of residents in the Richmond.

Neighbourhoods

Richmond District consists of five residential neighbourhoods: Lake District, Sea Cliff, Inner Richmond, Central Richmond and Outer Richmond.

Lake District

An affluent neighbourhood characterised by its many Victorian/Edwardian mansions, which is just south of Presidio of San Francisco and North of Inner Richmond. Its boundaries are: Presidio to the North, Arguello Boulevard to the East, California Street to the South, and 25th Avenue to the West. Its name is derived from Lake Street, the district's only main artery.

Sea Cliff

A small neighbourhood consisting mostly of exclusive mansions, some of which have unobstructed view of the Golden Gate Bridge. It gets its name as it sits along the North-western cliff of the Richmond District that borders the Pacific Ocean. Its boundaries are Pacific Ocean to the North, Presidio to the East, California Street to the Couth, and Legion of Honor to the West.

Inner Richmond

This area sits South of Lake District. Its boundaries are: California Street to the North, Arguello Boulevard to the East, Fulton Street to the South, and Park Presidio Boulevard to the West. The hub of Northern Inner Richmond is Geary Boulevard and Clement Street which are particularly known for Chinese, Cambodian, Korean, Burmese and Russian cuisine. The hub of Southern Inner Richmond is Balboa Street known for Japanese and Korean restaurants. Inner Richmond is a diverse neighbourhood with a sizable Chinese and Russian population.

Central Richmond

Located between Inner Richmond (to the East) and Outer Richmond (to the West). It is bounded by Park Presidio Boulevard to the East, California Street to the North, Fulton Street to the South and 33rd Avenue to the West. Its commercial strips are on Geary Boulevard and Clement Street (between 22nd to 25th Avenue). Central Richmond has a vast Chinese population and houses several top rated Chinese restaurants.

Outer Richmond

West of Central Richmond and bounded by Clement Street to the North, 33rd Avenue to the East, Fulton Street to the South and Ocean Beach to the West. It borders the Ocean Beach and the Cliff House, currently operating as a restaurant.

Streets

The Richmond District and the neighbouring Sunset District (on the south side of Golden Gate Park) are often collectively known as "The Avenues", because a majority of both neighbourhoods are spanned by numbered North-South Avenues. When the city was originally laid out, the avenues were numbered from 1st to 49th and the East-West Streets were lettered A to X. In 1909, to reduce confusion for mail carriers, the East-West Streets and 1st Avenue and 49th Avenue were renamed. The East-West Streets were named after Spanish explorers in ascending alphabetical order in a Southward direction. First Avenue was renamed Arguello Boulevard and 49th Avenue was renamed La Playa Street.

Today, the first numbered Avenue is 2nd Avenue, starting one block West of Arguello Boulevard, and the last is 48th Avenue near Ocean Beach. The Avenue numbers increase incrementally, with the exception that what would be 13th Avenue is called Funston Avenue named for Frederick Funston, a U.S. Army general.

Many of the East-West Streets are still named after the Spanish Conquistadors, but there are exceptions. The creation of Golden Gate Park took out the streets previously lettered E to G. The former D Street became Fulton, which is the Northern boundary of most of the Park.

North of the Park in the Richmond District, the streets are named Anza Balboa and Cabrillo.

Parks and Recreation
- Sutro Heights Park is located in Richmond District.
- Rochambeau playground. Located between 24th and 25th Avenue, the playground boasts tennis and basketball courts, as well as play structures.
- Lincoln Park and Golf Course in Outer Richmond which also contains the California Palace of the Legion of Honor.
- The former Fort Milley is now part of the Golden Gate National recreation area, a section of which contains a large Veterans Affairs Hospital.
- A small lake near Park Presidio and the Presidio Park forms part of the Mountain Lake Park.

RICHMOND, ILLINOIS, MCHENRY COUNTY

Richmond, IL was founded in 1844 by William McConnell who named the village after his childhood home in Richmond, Vermont. The population is about 1,016. There are still quite a number of old Queen Anne mansions and some have been converted into Bed and Breakfasts. Richmond lies almost at the Wisconsin border and is near Antioch, Illinois.

RICHMOND, INDIANA, WAYNE COUNTY, USA

Founded in 1806 by North Carolina Quakers, who settled along the White water River, Richmond is in Eastern Indiana near the Ohio border. The first settlers were John Smith and Jeremiah Cox. Smith named his settlement Smithville and Cox followed suit by calling his Jericho. However the other settlers did not take to either name and agreed on Richmond, county seat of Wayne County in 1873.

This Richmond served as a trade centre for travellers for many years, as well as being involved in agriculture and manufacturing. It also has the second oldest newspaper in the state, the Richmond Palladium. It has been nicknamed 'the Cradle of Recorded Jazz', 'the Lawnmower Capital' and 'the Rose City' at various times in its history, reflecting some of the industries in the town. Today Richmond is known for music, arts, historic architecture and is home to around 40, 000 people Glenn Miller Park Richmond, Indiana.

RICHMOND, FRANKLIN COUNTY

Established in 1857, located in the Kansas City metro area and has a population of around 500. The town itself was laid out as a railroad town in 1870. It was named after John C Richmond, an early settler from Ottawa who provided land for the railroad.

(With kind permission of richmond.org)

RICHMOND, KANSAS, NEMAHA COUNTY

This town has no remains and is now a ghost town. However it is reputedly a good place to hunt using metal detectors. It was once a way-station about three miles north of Seneca on the Oregon Trail, along the South Fork of the Nemaha River. It was an important stopping point along the road, but died when traffic later rerouted through Seneca.

RICHMOND, KENTUCKY, MADISON COUNTY

Founded in 1798 by Colonel John Miller, a soldier in the revolutionary war. According to tradition, Miller was attracted to the area by the good spring water and friendly Indians. That year, the Kentucky legislature approved moving the county seat from Milford to land owned by Colonel Miller. The residents of Milford adamantly opposed the move, which led to a fist fight between Dave Kennedy (representing Milford) and William Kearly (representing Richmond). Nevertheless, the county approved the move in March 1798. On July 4, 1798, the new town was named Richmond in honour of Miller's Virginia birthplace.

On August 30, 1862, during the Civil War, the Union and Confederate armies clashed in the Battle of Richmond. Troops under Confederate General Edmund Kirby Smith routed the soldiers of Union General William Nelson Out of Nelson's 6,500 men, only 1,200 escaped; the rest were all captured.

In 1906, Eastern Kentucky Normal School was founded in Richmond to train teachers. There were eleven members of the first graduating class in 1909. It became a four-year college in 1922 and added graduate programs in 1935. In 1965, the institution was renamed Eastern Kentucky University. In the late 1990s and through the first decade of the 21st century, Richmond had a commercial and residential boom.

Some facts:

- The population was 31,364 in 2010.
- Richmond is Kentucky's seventh-largest city (after Louisville, Lexington, Bowling Green, Owensboro, Covington, and Hopkinsville), the third largest city in the Blue Grass Region (after Louisville and Lexington), and the largest city between Lexington and Knoxville.
- Serves as the centre for work and shopping for South Central Kentucky.
- It is the principal city of the Richmond–Berea Metropolitan Area, which includes all of Madison and Rockcastle counties.

RICHMOND, MAINE, SAGADAHOC COUNTY

The area that later became Richmond was bought from the Indians in 1649 by Christopher Lawson and was one of the earliest settlements in Maine. Fort Richmond provided protection for the town from 1719 until 1755, when the forts Shirley, Western and Halifax were built further along the river. Indians attacked it twice, in 1722 and 1750.

What is now Richmond was part of Bowdoinham when it was incorporated in 1762. Richmond was incorporated in its own right on Feb 10 1823. Today it has a population of around 3,000.

Richmond Waterfront Park   Local neighborhood home

RICHMOND, MASSACHUSETTS, BERKSHIRE COUNTY

Richmond was incorporated in 1765 and named after Charles Lennox, Duke of Richmond. It is primarily an agricultural community and residential town, with many of the occupants commuting to nearby Pittsfield or having second homes in the area.

RICHMOND, MICHIGAN, MACOMB COUNTY

Settled in 1835 by Erastus Beebe, with his two brothers and several men from Richmond, Ontario County, New York and originally named Beebe's Corners. In five years the town was established and on 1 December 1859 the Grand Trunk Railway arrived. The town continued to flourish, ultimately joining forces with neighbouring towns Ridgeway and Cooper Town in 1878. The surrounding township had already been named Richmond in 1838 by settler Philip Cudworth and the combined town was incorporated as Richmond the following year.

The city is mostly in Macomb County with a small part in St Clair and has a population of around 5,000.

RICHMOND, MINNESOTA, STEARNS COUNTY

Named the 'Gateway to the Horseshoe Chain of Lakes', it was founded in 1856 and settled mostly by German immigrants. It was named after Cynthia Richmond, the wife of early settler and surveyor Reuben Richardson. The community is based around agriculture and the recreational opportunities provided by the lakes (more than 40 within 10 miles) and has around 1000 residents.

RICHMOND, MISSOURI, HOWARD COUNTY

The first settlers came from Virginia and named the town after the capital. It was already extinct many years before 1928.

RICHMOND, MISSOURI, RAY COUNTY

Located in Western Missouri just 7 Miles North of the Missouri River and 45 miles East of Kansas City. A rural community of 6,116 residents, it claims to be the 'Morel Mushroom Capital of the World'. Its festival, welcoming the coming of Spring, has been held in the first weekend of May for 25 years. *(Source: Richmond, Missouri Tourist Information)*

RICHMOND, NEW HAMPSHIRE, CHESHIRE COUNTY

The town's first charter dates to 1735 when Colonial Governor Jonathan Belcher granted it to soldiers returning from the war in Canada and it was named Sylvester-Canada. It was originally part of Massachusetts. New Hampshire ultimately became a separate province and the town was renamed Richmond and incorporated in 1752 by Governor Benning Wentworth. He named it after Charles Lennox, Duke of Richmond, a good friend of his.

(With kind permission of richmond.org)

RICHMOND, NEW YORK, STATEN ISLAND

Staten Island originally became the County of Richmond (along with Shooter's Island, and the islands of meadow on the West side of Staten Island) when it became part of the colony of New York on November 1, 1683. Richmond Town's central location linked the wide-spread farms of the Island and in the 1700s it became the government centre of the county. The town prospered in the early 1800s, but by the end of the century growth had slowed. In 1898 Staten Island became a borough of New York City and the government moved elsewhere.

Richmond Town then became the focus of historical preservation. The Staten Island Historical Society set out to preserve the declining town as a museum village. 'Historic Richmond Town' is now a museum and living history complex. The borough is co-extensive with Richmond County, and until 1975 the borough was officially named the Borough of Richmond. Staten Island has been sometimes called "the Forgotten Borough" by inhabitants who feel neglected by the city departments.

Some facts:

- The North Shore, especially the neighbourhoods of is the most urban part of the island; it contains the officially designated St. George Historic District and the St. Paul's Avenue-Stapleton Heights Historic District, which feature large Victorian houses.
- The East Shore is home to the 2.5-mile FDR boardwalk, the fourth-longest in the world.
- The South Shore developed rapidly beginning in the 1960s and 1970s, and is mostly suburban in character.
- The West Shore is the least populated and most industrial part of the island.
- Staten Island used to claim the largest landfill site in the world. It was closed in 2001, and then shortly afterward temporarily reopened to receive the debris from the September 11th attacks. The landfill is being made into what will be New York City's second largest public park.
- Staten Island is the only borough that is not connected to the New York City subway
- The free Staten Island ferry connects the borough to Manhattan and is a popular tourist attraction, providing views of the Statue of Liberty, Ellis Island and Lower Manhattan.

RICHMOND HILL, QUEENS, NEW YORK

Richmond Hill's name was inspired either by Richmond, London UK or because of Edward Richmond, a landscape architect in the mid-19th century who designed much of the neighbourhood. In 1868, a successful banker named Albon P. Man bought the Lefferts and Welling farms, and hired Richmond to lay out the community. Over the next decade streets, schools, a church, and a railroad were built, thus making the area one of the earliest residential communities on Long Island.

The area is well known for its large-frame single-family houses, many of which have been preserved since the turn of the 19th to 20th century. Many of the Queen Anne Georgian Homes of Old Richmond Hill still stand in the area today.

Richmond Hill first became developed in the later decades of the 19th century with the 1868 opening of the railroad station at the intersection of Hillside Avenue and Babbage Street, on the Montauk railroad line.

Between Long Island City and Eastern Long Island, Queens has population of over 2m and there are over 130 different languages spoken.

RICHMOND, NEW YORK, ONTARIO COUNTY

First settled around 1790 by Captain Pitts and James Codding. The town was established in 1796 as Pittstown, but was renamed Honeoye in 1808. In 1815, the name was changed to Richmond. One of the foremost farming towns in the county, it encompasses a number of small villages, of which Honeoye is the largest. Others include Richmond Center, Allen's Hill, Richmond Mills, and Dennisons' Corners.

RICHMOND, OHIO, JEFFERSON COUNTY

Richmond is a small village in Jefferson County. The land was bought by Joseph and Mary Talbott in 1808 and they arranged for it to be surveyed. By 1815 Main Street and four cross streets named Green, High, Walnut and Sugar had been laid out and the plots were then sold off.

The reason for the name Richmond is uncertain. Most likely it was named after Richmond, Virginia, but it may also have been after the Presbyterian Society Richmond Church which stood outside the town, or for a Richard Richmond who once worked for Mr Talbott. Descendants of the Talbott family still live in the village.

Ohio also has towns named New Richmond (Clermont County) and Richmond Heights (Cuyahoga County).

RICHMOND HEIGHTS, OHIO

Richmond Heights was originally founded as the Village of Claribel in 1917, but was later renamed as Richmond Heights in 1918.

Residential areas

Some popular developments include the Richmond Bluffs, near the Cuyahoga County airport, off Richmond Road; the Rushmore Subdivision off of Highland Road; Richwood, South of the Richmond-Highland Roads intersection. The largest residential area in Richmond Heights is the Scottish Highlands, off of Highland Road. Many ranch-style homes are found throughout the area. Many apartments are also located in Richmond Heights. Some major complexes are throughout the Loganberry section of Richmond Heights.

RICHMOND HEIGHTS, MISSOURI

This is a city in St Louis County, an inner-ring suburb of St Louis, Missouri. The 2010 census counted the population as 8,603. According to Robert L Ramsay professor of English at Missouri University who studied Missouri place names, the name was suggested by Robert E Lee who thought the topography of the area resembled Richmond, Virginia. In 2006, a joint study to consider the advantages and disadvantages of merging with the adjoining city of Clayton was under discussion.

RICHMOND HEIGHTS, FLORIDA

A 20th century development that addressed issues of lack of housing for African-American WWII veterans.

History

At the beginning of World War II, the United States Navy purchased 2,500 acres (1,000 hectares) of land in Southwestern Dade (now called Miami-Dade) County, Florida for the purpose of constructing an airship base. The land was owned by the Richmond Timber Company, a major supplier of Dade County Pine (a denser, harder, sub-species of Pinus Palustris, or Long Leaf Pine).

The base was named Naval Air Station Richmond, after the lumber company and was home to the 25 ships of ZP-21(Patrol, Airship Squadron 21 and Airship Wing 2). NAS RICHMOND was the second largest airship base in the United States, NAS LAKEHURST being the largest. NAS RICHMOND was destroyed by a hurricane and fire in September 1945.

The base was eventually home to 25 K-series blimps, three hangars, and 3,000 men. The hangars were 16 stories tall, built of Douglas fir brought in by train. The blimps protected ship convoys in the Florida Straits, and Richmond was the headquarters for the fight against Nazi U-boats operating in the Caribbean.

After the end of World War II, Captain Frank C. Martin, a white Pan-American pilot, purchased farm land adjacent to the base in rural southwest Dade County. With this purchase he created Richmond Heights, as a new community for returning African-American Veterans. Martin, who served with black soldiers in World War II, had gained great admiration and respect for their fighting spirit and ability to overcome many obstacles created by both war and racial prejudice.

Prior to the 1960's civil rights movement, decent affordable housing for African-Americans professionals in South Florida was difficult to find. Martin soon formed Richmond Development Inc., and sought the help of a local advisory committee of African-Americans to build his community. The committee included, Canon Theodore Gibson, Rector of Christ Episcopal Church in Coconut Grove, who was to become the leader of Miami's Civil Rights Movement; David A. Douglas, manager of the Atlanta Life Insurance Company and others such as Rev. Graham, Attorney G.E. Graves and Mr. William Perry.

Richmond Heights became the standard for developers, nationwide, to provide quality homes for African-Americans without skimping on land, materials, and labour. As for Martin he made his home available to residents for weekend social activities, where the subject often turned to his dream of building a community theatre and expanding the community across 152nd Street where lakes would be dug. Martin donated land for parks, two churches (Bethel Baptist & Martin Memorial A.M.E) and the elementary school, which today bears his name.)

By May 1951, Martin's Richmond Heights had 457 homes. Unfortunately, he did not live to see his dream community as Martin was killed in a collision with a truck when on a trip near Lake Placid in Central Florida,

Shocked at the loss of the 42-year-old community leader, construction stalled until 1952, when

Hialeah builder, E.J. Pollock, a good friend and believer in Martin's plan, purchased the remaining acreage and began building.

Today Richmond Heights is home to an average of 9,000 residents. Second, third, fourth and fifth generation descendants of the original community pioneers are ensuring the legacy of the historic neighborhood by continuing to move forward with a respect for heritage and an eye on the future.

RICHMOND, OKLAHOMA, WOODWARD COUNTY

This is a community located in Woodward County where there appears to be little or no development in the area.

RICHMOND, OREGON, WHEELER COUNTY

Richmond was formed in 1890 by a group of ranchers and farmers as a way to reduce the distance they had to travel to get supplies. It was named after the capital of the Confederacy. However, after around 30 years the availability of automobiles rendered its existence unnecessary as people could travel easily to larger towns nearby. Today Richmond is a ghost town.

RICHMOND, PENNSYLVANIA, PHILADELPHIA COUNTY

Originally the name of a tract of land in Northern Liberties Township, adjoining the Delaware River North of Ball Town and South of Point-No-Point. It was incorporated as a district on February 27, 1847. It extended along the Delaware River to a point some distance Northwest of the upper end of Petty's Island; then Northwest nearly to the point where Frankford Creek makes its most Southerly bend; thence Southerly bend; thence South-west to Westmoreland Street; Northwest along the same to Emerald Street; South-west along the latter to a lane running from Frankford Turnpike to Nicetown Lane; along Frankford Turnpike to the North boundary of Kensington District, and down the same to Gunners' Run, and along that stream to the Delaware River. The area was 1163 acres (4.7 km²). *(Source: Wikipedia)*

RICHMOND, RHODE ISLAND, WASHINGTON COUNTY

Rhode Island 35 miles South-southwest of Providence It is bordered to the North by the town of Exeter, to the West by the village of Wood River and to the South by the Pawcatuck River.

History

The area began existence as Narragansett County or Little Narragansett, after the indigenous people who lived there. Difficulty arose in the 1660s when it was claimed by Connecticut, Rhode Island (under two different charters) and a colony from Massachusetts. The King settled this in 1665 by dissolving all previous charters and making the area King's County – now Washington County. The town became called Westerly. Charlestown split off as a separate town in 1738; Richmond divided from Charlestown in 1747 and was incorporated as a town by the General Assembly of Rhode Island on August 18 that year.

The name of the town is said to derive from that of Edward Richmond, the state's Colonial Attorney General from 1677 to 1680. Tradition holds that the first settlers of Richmond were a married couple, John Babcock and Mary Lawson, whose son James was the first non-Native American child born in Narragansett territory. (The story is likely a later invention.)

Richmond's economy was based on textile manufacturing from the mid-1800s through the 1960s and has been rural and agricultural in nature. Since Interstate 95 was built many of the residents now work outside the town and today the town serves mainly as a bedroom community for commuters working in Providence, Warwick and Eastern Connecticut.

Richmond is a small town not easily travelled without a car, needed to visit the several villages that make up Richmond, including: Arcadia, Alton, Carolina, Hope Valley, Kenyon, Shannock, Usquepaug, Woodville and Wyoming.

Much of Richmond is still untouched by development. Indeed, Richmond is one of the last few enclaves that perpetuate the simple pleasures of Rhode Island.

Attractions near Richmond by car:

- Route 95 is the easiest way to get around, and the main highway for the area.
- University Of Rhode Island. Coming from 95 North, you must take exit 3A, and continue down 138 until it runs into URI. The speed limit is 35 for most of the way and the troopers are unforgiving, especially to out-of-state drivers.
- Hopkinton. When driving through town, go west on 138, which leads you into Hopkinton.
- Westerly. Get on 95 South until you get to Exit 1, which will lead you into Westerly.
- Getting to Warwick is just as easy, once you are on Main Street take 95 North, which will bring you to Providence, Warwick, and Massachusetts. There are many ponds and rivers where the nature enthusiast can enjoy fishing or kayaking.
- The Charlestown Fish Pond, a hidden treasure, is buried in the woods but still attracts up to 100 visitors at the start of every season.
- Crawly Preserve, a nature retreat, is located in Richmond.
- The North-South Trail runs through Richmond, with marked trails.
- Arcadia Management Area is a nice place for bike rides, hikes, walking dogs, kayaking,

hunting, and fishing. The small rivers and ponds throughout the area are stocked with trout every spring. Arcadia consists of 14,000 acres with cleared trails and a few different large ponds, the largest being Break Heart Pond.

- Washington County Fair. Held during the month of August in Richmond. For a week many gather to listen to music, watch racing lawnmowers, and to play carnival games. It's Richmond's biggest event, followed by the lively Farmers' Market in front of the Town Hall.
- Carolina Management Area is also a nice place to enjoy the outdoors. It consists of 2,359 acres of public property. The main access is located on the left hand side heading west on Pine Hill Road. It can be most easily accessed from Route 112, which is the main road that goes through the tiny hamlet of Carolina. This area has cut trails as well as a portion of the North-South trail going through the management area. Recreational activities include hiking, bird watching, hunting and fishing during the legal seasons, horse riding, and cross country skiing in the winter. (Camping is not permitted in any season, however.)
- With an abundance of rivers and streams, there are also plenty of good fishing spots in and around town. Supplies can be bought at the local bait and tackle shop in Hope Valley, a mile or so down Route 138 from the Town Hall.

RICHMOND, TEXAS, FORT BEND COUNTY

Although the first settlers came in 1822, the town was established by Robert Eden Handy and William Lusk in 1837 and named after Richmond, North Yorkshire. It was the first city incorporated by the Republic of Texas, briefly a country in its own right. In December that year it became the seat of government for Fort Bend County.

The population remained fairly static during most of its existence until commuters to Houston moved in after the 1950s. Richmond is considered the twin city of Rosenburg, as the cities' boundaries coincide: it also shares a boundary with Sugarland. In 2010, the US Census showed the city's population as 11,679. Even though it is the county seat, thus containing most of the local government offices, it actually is one of the smaller cities in the area. Adjacent Sugarland is the largest city in the county; Houston is not very far away so Richmond has expanded due to proximity.

History

In 1822, a group of Austin's colonists went up the Brazos River, stopping near present day Richmond where they built a fort called Fort Bend. Named after Richmond, England, the town was among the 19 cities first incorporated by the short-lived Republic of Texas, in 1837. Early residents of the city include many prominent figures in Texas lore such as Jane Long, Deaf Smith, and Mirabeau Lamar, who are all buried in Richmond. On August 16, 1889, the town was the site of the "Battle of Richmond," an armed fight culminating the Jaybird-Woodpecker War, a violent feud over post-Reconstruction political control of Fort Bend County. The Mayor from 1949 until his death in 2012 was Hilmar Moore.

Richmond is not sure if it wants to be a part of Houston's bustle or remain a slow-paced farm and ranch town. It tries to be both" and "It is part Acres' Homes, part Fort Bend County Fair." *(Source: Wikipedia and www.richmond.tx.nww.net)*

RICHMOND, UTAH, CACHE COUNTY

The original settlers in Richmond arrived in 1859, the first being Agrippa Cooper and his family. The actual town site was laid out in 1861 and it was incorporated as a city in 1868.
It is not known why the town was called Richmond. It may have been named after Richmond, Virginia, or the LDS Church apostle Charles C Rich or the deep rich mound of soil formed by the Cherry and City Creeks.

The population was 2,470 at the 2010 census. It is included in the Logan, Utah-Idaho Metropolitan Statistical Area. Part of the film 'Napoleon Dynamite' was filmed at Richmond.

RICHMOND, VERMONT, CHITTENDEN COUNTY

Located in the Western foothills of the Green Mountains on the Eastern edge of the Lake Champlain Valley. The Winooski River bisects the town of 4,090 residents from East to West, as does Interstate 89, the New England Central Railway and U.S. Route 2. The town was organized in 1795 and is recognized for being home to the National Historic Landmark Old Round Church, a 16-sided church built in 1813, considered to be among one of the first community churches in the country.

RICHMOND, WISCONSIN, SHAWANO COUNTY

The town was created on 25 Jan 1856. The Census of 2000 showed there were 1,719 people, 668 households, and 517 families residing in the town. The unincorporated communities of Red River and Thornton are located in the town.

RICHMOND, WISCONSIN, ST. CROIX COUNTY

The City of New Richmond, known as "The City Beautiful", is located in St. Croix County, Wisconsin, approximately 40 miles east of the St. Paul/Minneapolis Metro Area. The current population of New Richmond is 8,389. We are very proud of our "Main Street"- the window of our community. It provides an excellent setting for financial and professional services, shops and specialty stores. Our growing Business and Technical Park has several highly technical businesses and a Super Walmart. New Richmond offers one of the premier 27-hole golf courses in the state.

The New Richmond Municipal Airport is the 5th largest airport in Wisconsin. The Airport has 95 hangars. New Richmond Parks has 217 acres of park land and 10 miles of paved trails, six parks with play equipment, a camp-ground with eight sites that have full hook ups.

We live in a small town with big-city services. City Beautiful it is, in setting, in character, and quality of life!

Founded in 1858 and previously known as 'Cold Springs', New Richmond was originally settled in the 1850s where timber drove the early economy. As that resource was depleted, the community continued to thrive as a bustling business centre for the surrounding farmland. In June 1899, Wisconsin's deadliest tornado struck the city, which when combined with the fires that followed, left 117 dead and more than 200 buildings destroyed. Hard work and determination had most of the business rebuilt within six months. It was testimony to the spirit and fortitude of New Richmond's citizens, and a quality still seen in today's population – which was 1,556 at the 2000 census.

RICHMOND, WISCONSIN, WALWORTH COUNTY

Founded on Jan 12, 1841. The first settlers were Thomas James, Perry James and Robert Sherman, who came from Richmond, Washington County, Rhode Island.

The town population was 1,835 in 2000. The unincorporated communities of Lake Lorraine, Richmond, and Turtle Lake are located in the town.

RICHMOND HILL, GEORGIA

Richmond Hill was incorporated in March 1962. The current Mayor is Harold Fowler, who took office in 2009. The city is governed by a mayor and a four member city council.

Richmond Hill was the location of the discovery in 2004 of Benjamin Kyle, a man who suffers from retrograde amnesia as a result of a severe beating. He cannot remember who he is. As of June 2009, he remains unidentified.

In some respects, it might be helpful to differentiate between Richmond Hill City proper and the larger South Bryan County area. A large percentage of South Bryan residents live outside the city limits of Richmond Hill, especially in a number of planned developments east of the city along S.R. 144. This area contains large amounts of marsh and riverfront property, Fort McAllister Park, and the small community of Keller. Geographically, it is significantly larger than the municipal limits of Richmond Hill itself. However, the area contains no schools and few businesses or other public accommodations. As a result, residents of the entire South Bryan area rely on Richmond Hill proper for basic services, and must travel through the city to leave Bryan County, especially when commuting to Savannah Georgia via U.S. 17 or I-95. Most South Bryan residents, especially the large percentage of relative newcomers, would likely say they were "from Richmond Hill."

History

Richmond Hill has a historical connection to the industrialist Henry Ford who used the town, formerly known as Ways Station, as a winter home, and philanthropic social experiment, building the complex known as the Ford Farms along the Ogeechee River in the 1930s. After just one visit he chose this area as his Winter Home. Ford's dwelling was built on the site of Richmond Plantation, which was burned by elements of General William T Shermans's army at the conclusion of the "March to the Sea". Ford's holdings eventually totaled 85,000 acres (340km²) of agricultural and timber lands, most of which is now owned by the State of Georgia or ITT Ravonier, a timber company. Ford was also responsible for the construction of a number of public buildings:

- A kindergarten, which now houses the museum of the Richmond Hill Historical Society
- A chapel which now houses St. Anne's Catholic Church. Both are located on Georgia S.R. 144, also known as Ford Avenue within the Richmond Hill city limits.
- The Ford Plantation has now been redeveloped as a luxury resort, with vacation cottages, a clubhouse, tennis, and golf.

When it was suggested that the town be renamed with "Ford", Mr. Ford declined and instead Ways Station was renamed "Richmond Hill" after the site of Ford's home on the banks of the Ogeechee River.

Development

Real estate development in Richmond Hill has generally followed trends represented in the United States as a whole. Post Civil War populations remained relatively stable until the arrival of industrialist Henry Ford in 1930s. In the early 1970s, subdivisions began to spring up, and the "white flight" from nearby Savannah, GA began a settlement trend that has continued steadily until the present. Subdivisions of varying quality, ranging from starter homes to exclusive, gated golf communities, have emerged.

Schools

There are currently five public schools for people between the ages of 5-21 (21 in cases of challenged high-school students). The city is currently expanding its schools due to a large spike in population throughout the last ten years. Two new elementary and middle schools have just been built. Richmond Hill is expected to grow exponentially in the next few years.

Religion

There are over 20 churches of all denominations. Many of these organizations participate cooperatively in outreach programs that benefit the community as a whole. The Soup Kitchen aka Food for the Soul based out of the Richmond Hill United Methodist Church's kitchen is manned by ten separate churches rotating on a weekly basis, delivering over 350 hot meals to families in need within Richmond Hill.

The Way Station, another multiple church outreach program, has been in operation for over twenty years providing food, clothing, and other items that enhance the lives of families in the community.

Attractions

Richmond Hill hosts a number of community events at J.F. Gregory Park. Throughout the year the community comes together for supporting special events and causes, here are just a few: Annual Easter Extravaganza, Annual Memorial Day Observance, National Night Out, Old Time Family 4 July Festival & Fireworks, Annual Pumpkin Patch, Great Ogeechee Seafood Festival-35k attendees, Annual Veterans Day Observance, Matt Freeman Road Race and the Annual Chili Cook-off.

RICHMOND COUNTY, GEORGIA

It is one of the original counties of Georgia, created February 5, 1777. As of the 2010 population was 200,549. Following an election in 1995, the city of Augusta (the county seat) consolidated governments with Richmond County. The consolidated entity is known as Augusta-Richmond County, or simply Augusta. The cities of Hephzibah and Blythe in Southern Richmond County voted to remain separate and not consolidate. The county is part of the Augusta, Georgia Metropolitan area of Georgia and the county is named for Charles Lennox 3rd Duke of Richmond, a British politician and office-holder sympathetic to the cause of the American colonies. Richmond was also a first cousin to King George III. Richmond County was established in 1777 by the first Constitution of the (newly independent) State of Georgia. As such, it is one of the original counties of the state. It was formed out of a portion of the colonial Parish of St. Paul, after the Revolution disestablished the Church of England in the (former) Royal Province of Georgia.

Augusta National Golf Club, located in August Richmond County Georgia, is one of the most famous golf in the world. Founded by Bobby J ones and Clifford Roberts on the site of a former indigo plantation, the course was designed by Jones and Alister MacKenzie and opened for play in January 1933. Since 1934, it has played host to the annual Master Tournament, one of the four major championships in men's professional golf, and the only major played each year at the same course. It was the number one ranked course in Golf Digest's 2009 list of America's 100 greatest courses and is currently the number ten ranked course on *Golfweek Magazine*'s 2011 list of best classic courses in the United States, in terms of course architecture.

The golf club's exclusive membership policies have drawn criticism, particularly its refusal to admit black members until 1990, a former policy requiring all caddies to be black and its refusal to allow women to join. In August 2012, it admitted its first two female members, Condolezza Rice and Darla Moore. The golf club has defended the membership policies, stressing that it is a private organization.

RICHMOND COUNTY, NORTH CAROLINA

The county was formed in 1779 from Anson County. It was named for Charles Lennox 3rd Duke of Richmond. Kader Keaton, a Colonial American officer in the American Revolutionary War, was a founder of the Anglo-American settlement in Richmond County.

In 1899 the Southeastern part of Richmond County became Scotland County.

Railroad History

The city of Hamlet in the Southeastern sector of Richmond County is known for its railway history. Prior to the turn of the 20th century, the Seaboard Air Line Railroad moved to Hamlet, helping the town become a crossroads for rail spurs extending from Florida to New York and all points East and West. In 1900, the SAL Railroad constructed the Hamlet Historical Depot Seaboard Air Line Passenger Depot, a Victorian architectural train station which is one of the most photographed train stations in the Eastern United States. The depot was added to the National Register of Historic Places in 1971 and was fully restored in 2004.

In 2009, the city of Hamlet dedicated a new building to the Tornado steam engine locomotive—the first one in the State of North Carolina. The original locomotive was built in 1839 by D.J. Burr & Associates of Richmond, Virginia. It was briefly captured by Federal forces during the American Civil War before being repatriated. In 1892, the Tornado was featured in the Great Centennial Celebration of Raleigh, NC. Hamlet is also home to the National Railroad Museum and Hall of Fame, a striking collection of artifacts from the Seaboard Air Line Railroad spanning decades of time.

Sport

Richmond County is well known for its history in racing, with the advent of the Rockingham Speedway which opened in 1965. Until 2005, this one-mile race track featured bi-annual NASCAR-sanctioned events in the Spring Cup Nationwide series divisions. Presently, the race track hosts several other events hosted by sanctioning bodies including ARCA, USAR Pro Cup, and UARA Late Models.

- There is a weekly scheduled series of events for Bandolero and Legend's race car classes at the 1/2 mile infield track dubbed the "Little Rock".
- Richmond County also hosts lawnmower races. Each weekend from April–October, the Lion's Club of Ellerbe puts on a weekly show, attracting fans and competitors from surrounding counties and states.
- The County is also host to Rockingham Dragway, an international Hot Rod Association-sanctioned drag strip, which hosts over 90 drag racing events per year.

Attractions

Richmond County also has notable options for both fishing and hunting.

- Richmond County is home to the Sandhills Game Lands and the Pee Dee Wildlife refuge, where activities such as hiking, biking, horseback riding, boating, and hunting are available to the public. Popular hunting game include deer, turkey, quail, and fox squirrels.

- Blewett Falls is the largest lake in the county, offering fishing opportunities for Big Blue and Flathead Catfish as well as Striped Bass and Shad.
- Rockingham is working to develop a 10-mile "Blue Trail" for paddling and canoeing along Hitchcock Creek.

RICHMOND, KENTUCKY

The City of Richmond was founded in 1798 by Colonel John Miller, a soldier in the Revolutionary War. According to tradition, Miller was attracted to the area by the good spring water and friendly Native Americans.

That year, the Kentucky Legislature approved moving the county seat from Milford to land owned by Colonel Miller. Residents of Milford adamantly opposed the move, which led to a fist fight between Dave Kennedy (representing Milford) and William Kearly (representing Richmond). Nevertheless, the county approved the move in March 1798 and on July 4 that year; the new town was named Richmond in honor of Miller's Virginia birthplace.

On August 30, 1862, during the Civil War, the Union and Confederate Armies clashed in the Battle of Richmond. Troops under Confederate General Edmund Kirby Smith routed the soldiers of Union General William Nelson. Out of Nelson's 6,500 men, only 1,200 escaped; the rest were all captured. One historian called this battle *the nearest thing to a Cannae ever scored by any general, North or South, in the course of the whole war.*

In 1906, Eastern Kentucky State Normal School was founded in Richmond to train teachers. There were eleven members of the first graduating class in 1909. It became a four-year college in 1922 and added graduate programs in 1935. In 1965, the institution was renamed Eastern Kentucky University.

In the late 1990s and through the first decade of the 21st century, Richmond had a commercial and residential boom. Richmond is currently Kentucky's seventh-largest city, moving up four places from Kentucky's eleventh-largest city in the 2000 census.

RICHMONDS: CANADA

RICHMOND,, BRITISH COLUMBIA

Known as the *Island City, By Nature*, Richmond is a vibrant, multi-cultural community with sophisticated shopping, international cuisine and an abundance of recreational activities. Located just 20 minutes from down-town Vancouver, Richmond provides close access to Vancouver International Airport, the Gateway to the Pacific Rim and North America. Twenty minutes to the south is the BC Ferries Terminal and the Canada/US border at Douglas is only a thirty-minute drive away.

The first inhabitants of Richmond were the First Nations People, who thrived and lived close to the shore to harvest the abundance of fish. The first white settlers realized the great opportunities for farming due to the richness of the soil in the region. Before the first roads were built, the easiest form of transportation in the Fraser Estuary was by canoe and boat.

Early European and Asian settlers in the Fraser River Estuary quickly learned the importance of dike building to hold back both the ocean's high tides and the river's annual floodwaters. Much time and energy had to be spent diking and draining the low-lying land. Lulu Island, the largest in the delta and home to the city of Richmond, is embraced by all three arms of the Fraser River. Seven bridges and the George Massey Tunnel connect it to the rest of the Lower Mainland. Lulu Island is ringed by 48 miles (77 km) of dikes topped by easygoing walking and cycling trails. One of the first dike trails constructed in the Fraser Estuary was on Lulu's south shore at London's Landing. As these trails are level, you can cover a lot of ground in an outing while soaking up the island scenery.

The Fraser River's constant flow is responsible for filling in the shoreline of the Strait of Georgia with silt. Two expansive tracts of tidal marshland front the delta - Sturgeon and Roberts Banks - without providing much in the way of beaches. Instead, the shoreline is characterized by tall stands of bulrushes and lies strewn with driftwood.

Although Richmond has undergone a great deal of development, it continues to respect its roots as an agricultural community. Naturalists will want to explore Richmond's dyke trail system - perfect for cycling, jogging or leisurely walks, while others can enjoy a day of golf at one of the many fine golf courses.

Richmond takes great pride in its beauty, natural environment and numerous parks and gardens, and makes an effort to provide a welcome community in which people can visit, work and live.

Population: 176,599

Richmond is located west of Highway 99 on the Lower Mainland of BC, immediately south of Vancouver airport 12 miles (19 km) south of Vancouver.

Down on the south-western shore of Richmond sits historic Stevenson Village. At the turn of the century, Steveston was the busiest fishing port in the world. Now over 100 years old, Steveston has evolved into a picturesque working fishing village that comes to life each summer with plenty for visitors to see and do. Heritage sites, fresh seafood, great local restaurants and colourful gift shops and markets await the visitor.

- The Gulf of Georgia Cannery National Historic site in Steveston, on Fourth Avenue directly behind Canfisco, is operated by a group of community members and representatives of the local fishing industry and contains relics from the past, when the canneries operated day and night. A model of a 1930s production line is set up along one long L-shaped counter. Murals of fish and trawlers cover the walls; showcases full of glass net floats from Japan, various shiny salmon tins, and model boats help convey a sense of Steveston's heritage. Mountains of fishing gear and nets are arranged outside. The interpretive centre is open from May to mid-October. Admission includes a 20-minute film presentation in the Boiler House Theatre.
- In the heart old Stevenson you'll find the **Stevenson Museum**. Surrounded by board sidewalks, this former Northern Bank building reflects the community's heritage as a busy commercial centre.
- A treasure trove of classic motorcycles can be viewed at the **Trev Deeley Motorcycle Collection**, with over 250 motorcycles and 51 different makes on display. The collection is Trev Deeley's legacy of his involvement in the motorcycle, and includes British, American, Japanese, Italian and German motorcycles. Located at 13500 Verdun Place in Richmond, the collection is open Monday through Friday, 10am to 4pm. Admission is by donation, with proceeds donated to charity.
- Japanese and Chinese immigrants were among the first settlers to come to British Columbia, and this eastern influence has helped shape Richmond's development and culture. The most exquisite example of Chinese palatial architecture in North America exists at Richmond's magnificent **Buddhist Temple**.
- Also located in Steveston at the south foot of Railway Avenue is the **Britannia Heritage**

Shipyard. Visitors can take a self-guided walking tour of this National Heritage Site. Britannia is one of the few surviving examples from Steveston's rich past, when a mix of canneries, net lofts, boatyards, residences, and stores defined the neighbourhood. Restoration of the site is in the development stage, and over the coming years much of its former glory is slated to be restored. At present, the Britannia Shipyard augments a walking or cycling tour of the Steveston harbour. For more information, contact the Britannia Heritage Shipyard Society, (604) 718-1200.

- Time stands still as you venture through the doorway of the historic **London Heritage Farm**. Built during the 1890s, this fascinating heritage site on nearly 5 acres overlooking the south arm of the Fraser River offers the visitor a hands-on experience of rural life in the early development of Richmond. Surrounding the house are vagrant herb and flower gardens, and other attractions that include the restored Spragg family barn, and a hand tool museum.
- Some of the best live performances in the Pacific Northwest take place in the 560-seat **Gateway Theatre**, one of the most beautiful theatres in Canada.
- Known as *The Chapel in the Park*, **Minoru Chapel** was built in 1891 as the first church on Lulu Island, and is now a provincial heritage site functioning as an interdenominational chapel. Located in the heart of Richmond in **Minoru Park**.
- The **Richmond Library, Culture Centre, Art Gallery & Museum** is a popular multicultural complex featuring nine art studios, a gallery of contemporary art and an extensive museum housing over 9,000 artefacts. Collections include archaeology, ethnology, textiles, furnishings and items that reflect Richmond's diverse history.
- Nearly 43 percent of Richmond is preserved as farmland, bearing testimony to the city's rich agricultural heritage. The tradition continues with some of the finest **produce and fruit** crops in the world. During summer, visitors can sample and purchase a range of fruits, berries and vegetables at numerous farms, or visit one of the many famous **U-Pick farms**, harvesting their own bountiful crop.

Golf: The Richmond area offers a number of golf options:

- **Greenacres Golf Course** has earned the reputation for quality and excellence that few public courses can match. The beautiful 6,022-yard course is immaculately maintained, lined with lush trees with just enough water hazards and elevated greens to give anyone's game a good test. Open year round with a par 71 for men and a par 73 for women.
- **Mayfair Lakes Golf & Country Club** the West coast scenery, high standard in course conditioning, and beautiful surroundings combine to offer a world-class golf experience, conveniently located only minutes from the Vancouver airport.
- **Richmond Country Club** offers a championship golf course that entices both the avid and recreational golfer. The long fairways, manicured greens, and delightful vistas of woods and lakes serve to enhance this pleasure. Richmond Country Club's golf and racquet facilities are devoted to encouraging family participation.
- **Quilchena Golf and Country Club** prides itself in being a course of exceptional quality and playability for any level, offering 120 acres of golf with five sets of tees allowing for up to 6,665 yards of play.

Cycling: Two of the more popular starting points for a jaunt along the dike are:

- **Terra Nova**, at the north-western corner of Lulu Island. The Terra Nova trail-head is located at the west end of River Road. An observation platform and picnic tables are located nearby. At this point you can choose to head in several directions. If you want to explore the open marsh, take the 3-mile (5-km) West Dyke Trail. If you are more inclined to watch the action on the Fraser River, try the Middle Arm Trail, which runs an equal distance east along Moray Channel.

- **Garry Point Park**, on the south-western tip. Garry Point Park lies 3 miles (5 km) south of Terra Nova in the fishing community of Steveston. The park entrance and trail are located at the west end of Chatham Street. Take the Steveston Highway W exit from Highway 99 to reach Steveston.

- The **West Dyke Trail** connects Terra Nova with Garry Point Park. A cycle trip can just as easily begin from one point or the other. The **South Arm Dyke Trail** begins at the foot of No. 2 Road, just east of the Steveston harbour, and runs 3 miles (5 km) to Woodward's Landing Park beside the George Massey Tunnel and Hwy 99. Along the way, you'll pass numerous interpretive signs that outline interesting aspects of natural history, such as bird and fish migrations, as well as heritage sites. This section of trail offers a variety of stops for visitors to explore. You can pause for a look around at London Farms, picnic on the pier at the foot of No. 2 Road, and check out the old river homes on Finn Slough at the foot of No. 4 Road.

All trails are well signed with distances indicated in kilometres. The varied terrain of the Vancouver, Coast and Mountain region of BC accommodates every outdoor recreation.

Sea Island's back roads are a good place to cycle while watching planes or eagles, osprey, and heron, take off and land. A good place to begin is **Iona Beach Regional Park**. A causeway links Iona Island with Sea Island. Plan on taking 45 minutes or so to pedal the lengthy 7.5-mile (12-km) stretch of paved back roads that lead across Sea Island along Grauer, McDonald, and Ferguson Roads. If the back roads don't completely satisfy your will to wheel, tack on another 5.5 miles (9 km) by riding out to the end of Iona's jetty and back. By then you'll be saddle weary, for sure!

Fishing - McDonald Beach on Sea Island features a boat launch, a bait shop, and several picnic tables arranged on a high bank beside the Fraser River's North Arm. There's also fishing in near Steveston, where a municipal pier juts out into the Fraser at **Gilbert's Beach** beside the South Arm Dyke Trail at the foot of No. 2 Road, just east of the Steveston harbour. Anglers can catch salmon, trout, and numerous other species from the shores of Deas Island Regional Park. The Riverside picnic area is one of the most popular areas from which to fish. A *Tidal Waters Sports Fishing License* is required by all anglers and is available at most fishing shops. For more fishing information in British Columbia **Iona Island** offers 12 miles (20 km) of sandy shoreline beside Sea Island. Finding your way first crossing Sea Island, which can be tricky, as it is home to the Vancouver International Airport. As the back roads lead to Iona, you pass the somewhat misnamed **McDonald Beach**. At low tide a small beach is revealed here but it is hardly the place you'd want to spread out here on the western perimeter of the delta that defines Iona's unique personality. Two lengthy jetties shelter the beach as they stretch out into the Strait of Georgia. The banks of Iona Jetty are lined with concrete riprap, while North Arm Jetty is much sandier.

If you're looking for an ideal spot to do some **stargazing**, Iona Beach Park is it. The park is far away from the lights of nearby Richmond or Vancouver, and out here the night sky is as black as bean sauce. Just make sure that you leave your vehicle outside the nearby gates if you plan to be in the park after closing time, unless you're attending one of the special stargazing evenings offered throughout the year by GVRD Parks. Note: Although the gates to the park close at dusk, visitors may still enter on foot.

Photography - Plexiglas shelters are located at the midway point and the far end of the pipeline at Iona Beach Regional Park. Not only do they provide a break from the cool winds that often blow across the ocean, but these are also ideal locations from which to snap a sunrise or sunset shot. The most prominent features in the panoramic vista are Mount Baker to the east, the Coast Mountains to the north with Pacific Spirit Regional Park in the foreground, and the open water of the Strait of Georgia with a profile of the Vancouver Island Mountains to the west.

The estuary dike trails in Iona Beach Regional Park provide excellent and extended leisurely **walking trails** and jogging opportunities.

- Covering over 200 acres of parkland, the unique **Richmond Nature Park** covers one of the last remnants of Lulu Island's once-extensive bogs. Visitors can pick and choose from the network of trails winding through the bog and shady birch forest, viewing the wonderful variety of birds and wild flowers.
- The **Salmon Festival**, held here on July 1st, is a cultural celebration and taste   sensation that can't be missed.
- Don't miss the **Cranberry Harvest and Slugfest**, held annually in Richmond Nature Park during October.

Circle Tour: See the best of the area on a driving Circle Tour. Head north out of Vancouver for a scenic tour of the Sunshine coast and Vancouver Island or stay on the intensely scenic Sea to Sky Highway, passing through the magical winter resort town of Whistler and looping through the Coast mountains To explore the rural farmlands and forests of the fertile Fraser Valley travel outbound on the scenic route north of the historic Fraser River, returning westwards along the Trans Canada a towel (the wake put up by passing marine traffic on the Fraser River would soon send you running for higher ground). Iona Beach Park is really where you want to head to if you are looking for a place to stretch out beside some driftwood. *(With kind permission of Tourismrichmond)*

RICHMOND, ONTARIO

A small village in South-Eastern Ontario spanning the Jock river, a tributary of the Rideau River it was selected by the British Army in 1818 as the site for the area's first military settlement and was named after the Duke of Richmond, who was the newly appointed Governor General of the Upper Canadas.

History

After the War of 1812, loyal settlers were sought for Upper Canada (now Ontario). The United Empire Loyalists, who, after the American Revolution, had helped to settle areas further South and West in Upper Canada were being regarded with increasing suspicion.

Instead, disbanded soldiers were the most immediate loyal settlers for this new era of development. Richmond was selected by the British Army in 1818 as one of the first military settlements (others included Perth and Lanark). The village was laid out in a grid on the North bank of the Jock River (which for a while was renamed the Goodwood after the Duke's English estate). Richmond was the centre for the administration of lands in the area. Military supervisor, Major Burke, placed mainly Irish soldiers of his 99th Regiment in Goulbourn. Scottish settlers from Perthshire were placed in the adjoining area of Northeast Beckwith, while Irish civilians were settled in Southeast Beckwith, Goulbourn, and parts of neighbouring townships.

In the spring of 1818 the officers and men of 99th were at Quebec, and, in common with those of other regiments, had their choice of a passage home to Ireland or, if they so elected, to remain here in Canada where they would receive free grants of land in the new country to be settled on the Ottawa and Rideau rivers. Thus, in late 1818 (with the help of neighbours in Hull, Quebec assisting in construction) the village of Richmond was born.

From 1818 to 1822, the village was managed by the Settling Branch of Upper Canada's Military Department. Village life was dominated by military culture and institutions during these early years. While official plans of the village demonstrate optimism for its future growth and importance, this never came to pass. By the time the military relinquished control of the village in 1822, very few civilians had settled. Many historians argue that the highly planned villages of early nineteenth century Ottawa Valley were a failure compared to villages and towns that sprang up in a more "organic" nature in response to such factors as proximity to transportation routes, natural resources, and quality farm land. In the case of Richmond, the rising importance of Bytown and the building of the Rideau Canal several kilometres east of Richmond significantly contributed to its failure to thrive.

By 1832, Hamnett Pinhey described the state of Richmond to the Freeholders of Carleton as, "a jail in itself." He goes on to note that, *"I have known that place these thirteen years, it was then a rising place, but it has been falling ever since, and is now almost nothing; not a house has been built but many a one has fallen down and still are falling. . . if you get into it in the Spring, you can't get out till Summer; and if you get into it in the Fall, you must wait till the Winter, and whose fault is it but the Magistrates and Gentry of Richmond; that is to say the Shopkeepers?"*

Richmond was incorporated as a village in 1850 and was annexed by Golbourn Township in

1974. In 1969, Richmond became part of Regional Municipality of Ottawa Carleton until 2001. It has been within the City of Ottawa since January 1, 2001 as one of the many rural villages recognized by the City of Ottawa. Each of these amalgamations has resulted in a significant reduction in democratic representation for villagers. Some residents in Richmond are displeased about the most recent amalgamation into the Ottawa city structure and would like to de-amalgamate along with other areas of rural Carleton County.

Richmond's amalgamation into the city of Ottawa is a cause for concern for many local residents. Amalgamation has also gained the attention of several researchers concerned with sustainable community development and local governance. David Douglas' study of restructured rural communities points out that threats to local traditions and values, lack of local control over the restructuring process, and a marked decrease in democratic representation are some of the important issues that have been neglected through this process and which pose a significant threat to the health and liveability of amalgamated rural communities such as Richmond. Contained within the City of Ottawa structure, Richmond is vulnerable to many of Douglas' concerns.

Other facts:

- The village mascot is a fox, after a local legend relating to a rabid fox that is reported to have been responsible for spreading the disease to the Duke of Richmond's dog, which subsequently bit the Duke, killing him.
- The village of Richmond has many historical buildings such as St Philip's Church, which is the oldest church in the Catholic Archdiocese of Ottawa.
- The Canadian 2006 Census showed a population of 3,301.
- Richmond is 15 km from North Gower, 32 km from Carleton place, 36 km from Downtown Ottawa, 41 km from smiths fall and 45 km from Perth.
- The Rideau Trail, a hiking trail, runs through Richmond.
- The town's motto is *En la rose, je fleuris* (French for "Like the rose, I flourish"), reflecting either the motto of the Duke of Richmond, or the fact that the town was a centre of rose-growing in the early 20th century. At that time, it was known as the "Rose Capital" of Canada.
- A more recent motto for Richmond Hill is *A little north, a little nicer.*

RICHMOND, CALGARY, ALBERTA

Richmond is a suburb of Calgary in the South West of the City with about 3,400.

Calgary is situated on the Bow River in the South of the province; it's an area of foothills and prairie approximately 50 miles East of the front ranges of the Canadian Rockies. The city is located in the grassland and parkland natural regions of Alberta. The 2011 census indicated there was a population of 1,096,833 and a metropolitan population of 1,214,839, making it the largest city in Alberta, and the third largest municipality and fifth largest metropolitan area in Canada.

Calgary is designated as a Global City and was cited by the Brookings institution as one of the top 200 cities worldwide with a top performing local economy for 2011. The city was ranked first nationally, and 51st in the world, in that aspect. Additionally, Calgary was voted third in quality of life among North American cities by the 2011-2012 issue of American Cities of the Future.

Calgary's economy is decreasingly dominated by the oil and gas industry, although it is still the single largest contributor to the city's GDP. As of 2010, the city had a labour force of 618,000 (a 74.6% participation rate) and 7.0% unemployment rate. In 2006, the unemployment rate was amongst the lowest of the major cities in Canada at 3.2%, causing a shortage of both skilled and unskilled workers.

Numerous films have been shot in the general area. The television film Cross Trail (2001), starring Tom Selleck, was shot on a ranch near Calgary, though the stated setting of the film is Wyoming.

Attractions

- Heritage Park Historical Village depicts life in pre-1914 Alberta and features working historic vehicles such as a steam train, paddle steamer and electric streetcar. The village itself comprises a mixture of replica buildings and historic structures relocated from Southern Alberta.
- Canada Olympic Park, which features Canada's Sports Hall of Fame and Spruce Meadows.
- There are many shopping areas in the city centre, as well large suburban shopping complexes in the city. Among the largest are Chinook Centre and Southcentre Mall in the South, Westhills and Signal Hill in the Southwest, South Trail Crossing and Deerfoot Meadows in the Southeast, Market Mall in the Northwest, Sunridge Mall in the Northeast, and the newly built CrossIron Mills just North of the Calgary city limits, and South of the City of Airdrie.

Sports and recreation

In large part due to its proximity to the Rocky Mountains, Calgary has traditionally been a popular destination for winter sports. Since hosting the 1988 Winter Olympics, the city has also been home to a number of major winter sporting facilities at Canada Olympic Park (bobsleigh, luge cross country skiing ski jumping downhill skiing snow-boarding, and some summer sports) and the Olympic Oval speed skating and hockey. These facilities serve as the primary training venues for a number of competitive athletes. Also, Canada Olympic Park serves as a mountain biking trail in the summer months.

In the summer, the Bow River is very popular among fly fishermen. Golfing is also an extremely popular activity for Calgarians and the region has a large number of courses.

Calgary hosted the 2009 World Water-Ski Championship Festival in August, at the Predator Bay Water-Ski Club which is situated approximately 40km (25 mi) south of the city.

In July 2012, the Calgary Stampede Round 3 saw Richmond v Western Bulldogs to celebrate a 100 years of the Stampede Rodeo.

RICHMOND, QUEBEC

Named after the 4th Duke of Richmond, who died and was buried there in 1819.

In 2011, it had a population of 3,275. The town nestles amidst rolling farmlands on the Saint-François River between Sherbrooke and Drummondville, in the heart of Estrie. A French-speaking town as many in Quebec are.

RICHMOND, PRINCE EDWARD ISLAND, PRINCE COUNTY

A small village in the West part of Prince Edward Island. It was incorporated in 1979 and has a population of a few hundred people. It is famed for the Richmond Dairy Bar.

A farming area west of Summerside, the community is situated on Route 2 and until 1989 was served by CN Rail.

RICHMOND HEIGHTS, SASKATOON

Adjacent to the South Saskatchewan River, Richmond Heights features walking trails in the Meewasin Valley.

Land was annexed for the Richmond Heights in 1955-59. The majority of dwellings were part of the original construction which took place in the 1960s. In 2006, the average home size was 2.3 residents and about 950 people live in the town.

Within the Lawson Suburban Develoment Area (West Side), the neighbourhood of Richmond Heights is bordered on the North by Circle Drive, Warman Road lies to the West side. To the South is Hazen Street, and finally the Eastern perimeter is the geophysical boundary of the South Saskatchewan upon which G.D. Archibald Park North (which hosts baseball and soccer games) is found.

There are now no schools here. In the 1970s, Richmond Heights School served children in the neighborhood before closing in the mid-1980s due to declining enrolment. The building is now the Luther Senior's Centre with a senior's residential complex to the East on the old playground site.

RICHMONDS: NEW ZEALAND

RICHMOND, NELSON PROVINCE, SOUTH ISLAND

The first settlers were surveyors T. J. Thompson and J. W. Barnicoat in June 1842. It was named Richmond in 1846, on the suggestion of George Snow, one of the early residents who came from Richmond upon Thames, Surrey.

Nelson is New Zealand's top holiday spot, with the highest number of sunshine hours anywhere on both islands. Richmond is a small town, about 15 minutes from Nelson City and is surrounded by beaches, farmland and the Mount Richmond State Forest Park. It is 30 mins from the Abel Tasman National Park.

The Census conducted on 6 March 2006 counted more than 14,000 residents. Although it lies outside the boundaries of Nelson City, it forms part of the Nelson Urban Area for statistical purposes, and New Zealanders informally consider it part of Greater Nelson or the "Top of the South". The two unitary authorities co-operate for tourism -marketing purposes via "Latitude Nelson".

Richmond is the main shopping and business precinct in the District and in recent years it has been transformed with the addition of many new retail outlets and the largest Mall in the top of the south. Richmond has a comprehensive shopping area and a good choice of eating places, all with free parking.

Despite continued growth, Richmond has managed to retain its family-friendly 'small town' feel. It is now a favourite stopping place for the thousands of tourists that visit Tasman District and offers a great network of green spaces and walking tracks to enjoy.

Attractions
- Richmond is surrounded by national parks, Abel Tasman National Park, Nelson Lakes National Park and Kahurangi National Park.
- Waterways Rabbit Island (Moturoa), Aniseed Valley, Waimea River and Kaiteriteri.

(Source: http://www.nelsonnz.com/nelson-richmond)

[I have 3 cousins who live North Island and they all say how lovely Richmond, Nelson is. BS]

RICHMOND, CANTERBURY, CHRISTCHURCH

Canterbury is New Zealand's largest region by area with an area of 45,346km² and has an estimated population of 558,800 (June 2012), making it the largest region in the South Island and the second largest region in New Zealand by population.

Richmond suburb is situated to the inner North East of the city centre, bounded by Shirley Road to the North, Hills Road to the West, Gloucester Street to the South and the Avon River to the east. It has a population of about 5400 people.

The region is traditionally bounded in the North by the Conway River and to the West by the Southern Alps. The southern boundary is the Waitiki River. The area is commonly divided into North Canterbury (north of the Rakaia River to the Conway River), Mid-Canterbury (from the Rakaia River to the Rangitata), South Canterbury (South of the Rangitata River to the Waitaki River) and Christchurch City. For many purposes South Canterbury is considered a separate region centre on the city of Timari.

RICHMONDS: AUSTRALIA

RICHMOND, NEW SOUTH WALES

Originally the home of the native Darug people, British settlers arrived in 1789. Today Richmond's main businesses are agriculture and aviation. It is located on the outskirts of the Sydney area.

History

The area was known by British settlers as 'Richmond Hill'. This name was given by Governor Phillip, in honour of Charles Lennox, the third Duke of Richmond who was Master General of Ordnance in the Pitt administration.

The local area was the third area to have European settlement in Australia after Sydney and Parramatta. The first 22 European settlers came to the area in 1794 to farm a total of 30 acres (12 ha) in what is now Pitt Town Bottoms. They needed good farming land to help overcome the desperate need for food in the new colony. By 1799 this region was producing about half the grain produced in the colony.

The Battle of Richmond Hill took place in May and June 1795 between the Darug people and the European settlers. It is perhaps the first time that the colonial authorities sent in the troopers and expressly stated their intent to 'destroy' the whole local Aboriginal population of an area.

Around 1811, Macquarie established the five Macquarie Towns in the area: Windsor, Richmond, Castlereagh, Wilberforce and Pitt Town. One of the early settlers, James Blackman, built Bowman Cottage from brick nog, a common construction technique in the colony, using money borrowed from William Cox. The house was constructed between the years 1815 and 1818. James was unable to pay his debts and was forced to sell the property to George Bowman. The building was restored by the NSW Public Works Department and then became a Division of the Australian Foundation for the Disabled, providing employment for the disabled.

During WWII the RAAF operated a top secret operations bunker from somewhere in Richmond. It was either half or completely underground. The location of this bunker is unknown but it has been reported that this bunker was identical to the Bankstown Bunker which is currently buried under a public park in Bankstown. It has also been reported that this bunker could still be intact.

RAAF Base Richmond is a Royal Australian Air Force base at Richmond which was established in 1923. The air base is currently the home to the RAAF's transport squadrons. During the Vietnam War, logistic support and medical evacuations were supplied by the C-130 Hercules aircraft from RAAF Richmond.

Richmond has a range of educational facilities, from primary and high schools to Technical and Further Education (TAFE) and university campuses.

Geography

The expansion of the Sydney suburban area has almost reached Richmond and it is now considered to be an outer suburb of Sydney. Bells Line of Road which leads into, over and across the Blue

Mountains, finishing in Lithgow, starts in Richmond. Richmond railway station is the terminus of the Richmond branch of the Western Line of the CityRail network.

Richmond is surrounded by the 329km² Richmond Woodlands Important Bird Area, identified as such by BirdLife International because of the importance of the patches of remnant eucalypt woodland it contains for endangered Regent Honeyeaters and Swift Parrots. *(Source: Wikipedia)*

RICHMOND, QUEENSLAND

Located on the Flinders Highway, 498 km west of Townsville and 406 km east of Mount Isa. It is the administrative centre of the Richmond Shire. In 2006 it had a population of 554 according to the Census.

The Flinders River forms the northern boundary of the town. Traditionally, the two biggest industries in Richmond are sheep and cattle-farming, however tourism is an increasingly important aspect of the local economy. In addition to being a major transit stop on the Flinders Highway, recent paleontological discoveries have unearthed the fossils of prehistoric marine creatures, some of which are on display in Richmond.

Facilities

Richmond has a public library, golf course, bowling club, swimming facilities, race course, caravan park, tourist information centre and a fossil museum named Kronosaurus Korner.

RICHMOND, TASMANIA

A town about 25km north-east of Hobart, in the Coal River region, between the Midland Highway and Tasman Highway, with a population of 880 (206 Census). It was initially part of the route between Hobart and Port Arthur until the Sorell Causeway was constructed in 1872.

Some facts:

- Richmond's most famous landmark is the Richmond Bridge, built in 1823 to 1825, around the time of the town's first settlement. It is Australia's oldest bridge still in use.
- St John's Catholic Church was built in 1836, and is considered the oldest Roman Catholic Church in Australia.
- Present-day Richmond is best known as being preserved as it was at that time. It is a vibrant tourist town, with many of the sandstone structures still standing.
- Richmond Post Office opened on 1 June 1832.
- Notable tourist attractions are the Richmond Gaol, Zoodoo Wildlife Park, a model of Old Hobart Town in the 1800s, and numerous old and heritage-listed buildings and parks.

Tasmania

Abbreviated as Tas and known colloquially as "Tassie" is an island state, part of the Commonwealth of Australia, located 240 kilometres to the South of the Australian continent, separated by Bass straits. The state includes the island of Tasmania, the 26th largest island in the world, and there are 334 surrounding islands.

In 2010 the state's population was 507,626, of whom almost half reside in the greater Hobart precinct. Tasmania is promoted as the *natural state*, the "Island of Inspiration and *A World Apart, Not A World Away* owing to its large and relatively unspoiled natural environment. Almost 37% of Tasmania lies in reserves, national parks and World Heritage Sites. The island is 364 kilometres long from its Northernmost to Southernmost points, and 306 kilometres from West to East.

The state capital and largest city is Hobart. Boundary Islet, a nature reserve in Bass Strait is the northernmost terrestrial point of the state of Tasmania which, due to a quirk of history, is shared with the state of Victoria.

RICHMOND, MELBOURNE, VICTORIA

Richmond is a suburb of Melbourne, 3 km South-East from Melbourne's Central Business District, with a population of 26,121 (2011 Census). Richmond was named after Richmond Hill, London, with its outlook of the river bend (Yarra); however the waterfront area was later named Cremorne, though it is not known why or when.

Some facts:

- The suburb's Local Government Area is the City of Yarra municipality.
- Richmond is well known for its vibrant and popular Little Saigon area along Victoria Street.
- Victoria Gardens Shopping Centre is a large modern complex built in 2001 to service the Inner Eastern suburbs.
- The Royal Studley Hotel was built in 1891 and is now used as a home-wares shop.
- Richmond Power Station was built in 1891.
- The Burnley Theatre is now a commercial home wares shop, but contains some elements of the original interiors, including the foyer and stage.
- 450 Swan Street, completed in 1995, combines an old bank and modern building in an outstanding example of de-constructivist architecture, by Ashton Raggart McDougall.
- Richmond Town Hall is a landmark building currently operated by the City of Yarra, which was built in the 1880s and redecorated during the inter-war years.
- Hotels include The Mountain View Hotel, Corner Hotel, Great Britain Hotel, The Rising Sun and The Swan (1890) and many others known for their live music.

Richmond does have some parks and gardens and reserves, however, they are notably absent in the main centre of the suburb.

- The largest park is Citizens' Park (Richmond Oval), bordering on Church and Highett Streets.
- Other notable spaces include Barkly Gardens and the Allen Bain Reserve, as well as a number of smaller parks and reserves.
- Other large parks are located in nearby suburbs, including Yarra Park and Melbourne Park in East Melbourne (Jolimont), the Golden Square Bicentennial Park, Burnley Park and Oval, the Burnley Golf Course (survey paddock) and a number of sport reserves and ovals in neighbouring Burnley.
- Pridmore Park, Yarra Bank Reserve, Creswick Street Reserve and St James Park are in Hawthorn.
- Dickinson's Reserve, Yarra Bend Park, Studley Park Golf Course and Studley Park are in Kew. The latter two are named after Studley Park, Ripon, North Yorkshire, near Richmond.

Religion

Australia is home to diverse faiths and Richmond is no exception.

- The local large Catholic community is served by St Ignatius' Church on Church Street and St James Parish.
- Anglicans also have a presence in Richmond, served by St Stephens, next door to St Ignatius' Church.
- A Uniting Church also serves its members with a Fijian presence, located on Church Street.
- Due to a large number of Greek immigrants there is a Greek Orthodox Church, located on Burnley Street, which is open for mass every Sunday and brings together Richmond's Greek Community.
- There is also a large Assemblies of God Church, Richmond AOG, in Griffiths Street.

Sport

Richmond is home to the Richmond Football Club, an Australian Rules football club, which is a member of the Australian Football League. Richmond is one of the most successful football teams in Australia, having won 10 premierships in the VFL/AFL. The club has a cult following not only in Richmond, but throughout the eastern suburbs of Melbourne.

The Tigers play home games at the Melbourne Cricket Ground located just outside the suburb's border, which regularly attract crowds in excess of 40,000. However, it can draw crowds as large as 80,000 against fierce rivals. Richmond is also the home to Richmond Soccer Club, which currently play in the Victorian Premier League. They play their home matches at Kevin Bartlett Reserve in Burnley. The ground is named after Richmond Australian Rules footballer Kevin Bartlett, who was the first VFL player to play 400 senior games.

Transport

Richmond has an established transport system involving arterial roads, five train stations, seven tram routes, a bus route and a series of bicycle trails, including the Capital City Trail and the Yarra River Trail. The main train station in Richmond is Richmond railway station. It is an interchange for all metropolitan passenger trains to the Eastern and South-Eastern suburbs. Railway lines that travel through Richmond Station include the Pakenham, Cranbourne, Frankston, Lilydale, Belgrave, Glen Waverley, Sandringham and Alamein lines.

RICHMOND RIVER, NEW SOUTH WALES

The river rises in the great dividing range on the southern slopes of Mcpherson Range, West of Mount Lindesay, and flows generally South East and North East, joined by twelve tributaries including the Wilsons River, before reaching its mouth at its confluence with the Coral Sea of the South Pacific Ocean near between Ballina descending 840 feet over its 147 mile course. The catchment area of the river is estimated at 6,862 square kilometers (2,649 sq miles), which makes it the sixth largest catchment in New South Wales. Its floodplain has an area of over 1,000 square kilometers (390 sq miles).

Aboriginal history

The traditional custodians of the land surrounding the Richmond River are the Aboriginal people of the Bundalung Clan, whose territory reached north to the current city of Toowoomba and included the current towns of Tenterfield and Warwick. One of the annual rituals of the Bundalung people was the movement from the mountain ranges to the coast during the winter months, when the mullet were plentiful.

European history

Omitted by Captain James Cool when he sailed up the East coast of the Australian mainland in 1770, it wasn't until Captain Henry John Rous identified the mouth of the river in 1828 that it was discovered by Europeans. Rous entered the river and sailed about 20 miles (32 km) up river. He subsequently named the river Richmond after The Fifth Duke of Richmond. Later that year the explorer Allan Cunningham reached the river by land.

The river was a major port from the 1840s until well into the 20th century. Soon after the first white settlers arrived they discovered the abundant supply of Australian Red Cedar in the Richmond Valley and immediately began logging. The river was vital in the transportation of this resource.

At the time of its discovery in 1828 and until the late 1890s the river had a treacherous mouth of shifting sand bars, and many ships and lives were lost on it. Understandably, a decision was made to construct two breakwaters to channel the river's flow and these were completed in the early 1900s. The construction of the breakwaters also led to the formation of Shaw's Bay (after sand built up behind what is now called Lighthouse or Main Beach).

In 1846, a conflict between white settlers and local Aborigines flared up in the river valley: the Richmond River Massacre caused the deaths of around 100 of the latter.

With the decline of shipping as a transport mode, owing to better roads and rail, and the closing of the North Coast Steam Navigation Company (the major shipping firm of the area) in 1954, the river became less important as a port.

Current usage

For boats, the river is navigable for a short way up its length, possibly as far as Casino. Wilsons River, which flows through the city of Lismore and is a major tributary of the Richmond, is navigable at least as far as Boatharbour, approximately 12 kilometers (7.5 miles) upstream from Lismore.

The Richmond River is heavily used for irrigation along its length. Several weirs have been constructed in order to mitigate the effects of flooding, most notably at Casino.

RICHMONDS: SOUTH AFRICA

RICHMOND, CAPE PROVINCE

A small village with a kaleidoscopic past: the quiet, almost genteel air of remote little Richmond with its 19th century buildings masks a past when for a few fleeting moments it was part of world history in the making. A boy born here went on to become the acknowledged father of modern orthopaedic surgery. And then, years later, fierce fighting gained it a niche in the history of the last of the gentlemen's wars.

There is even a strong link with the devastating potato crop failure in Ireland in 1859, when people fled the famine. One of these thousands was an exceedingly able school teacher who created the sound basis for schooling in Richmond. International links extend also to horse-breeding circles in Kentucky in the United States. The local museum is one of only two in the world to honour the saddle-horse breed. Also, the town was named in honour of an English Duke.

Early History

Richmond was established on one of the highest and coldest parts of the Cape's inland plateau in 1843. In common with most Karoo towns, it was founded to meet the religious needs of a growing farming community, but to a large extent that is where the similarity ends. Unlike most others, it was built astride a river, the reason for the irregular street grid. Also, the church was not built as the village focal point: the centrepiece is the village square.

People who moved northwards to settle in the Karoo relied on daily Bible readings or travelling preachers for religious needs. Churches were vast distances away, and most farmers could not leave their farms unprotected. Daily hardships also often thrust religious instruction aside. The need to establish a village became pressing. So, when official permission was granted, community leaders met and Driefontein, the farm of P J van der Merwe, was chosen as a suitable site. It lay on the banks of the Ongers River with its reliable source of fresh water from the three fountains from which the farm took its name. To this day, water still bubbles from these fountains in the Wilgersloot (Willow Stream) area. Driefontein was acquired towards the end of 1843. In those years, the area was rich in game and lions roamed the banks of the Ongers River to prey on buck coming to drink.

In Honour of a Duke

Early in 1844, the townsfolk approached the new Governor of the Cape, Sir Peregrine Maitland, who took office that year, for permission to name their village in his honour. He declined, and suggested that it rather be named after his father-in-law, the Duke of Richmond. So it was officially named Richmond in October, 1845 much to the delight of Sir Peregrine's wife and her father.

The first plots were officially sold by auction after the "nagmaal" (Holy Communion) service on April 19, 1845. All plots were sold on condition that no strong liquor be brewed or sold on the premises. The town become a magisterial district in 1848 and a municipality in 1854.

Irish Connection

After the disastrous failure of the potato crop in Ireland in 1859, Helena Broadbrook and her brother decided to emigrate. They were welcomed to South Africa by Arthur Gilstain, whom she later married on January 18, 1860. They moved to Richmond where Helena became governess to the children of the two doctors. One of these children was Emil Hoffa, destined to become world famous.

Helena, born in 1837 in Mullengar, West of Dublin, started a school in Paul Street. She was a qualified teacher, could speak English, French and German, and had travelled widely in Europe as a companion to the wife of Sir William de Salis, a Royal Navy admiral. Helena spent a year with this noble lady in Switzerland helping her to recover from the loss of twin sons. As a pastime she translated German Fairy Tales into English. When diamonds were discovered, Arthur Gilstain, once accused of stealing a kiss from the lovely Juana, Spanish wife of Sir Harry Smith, left for Kimberley to try his luck at the diggings. On the eve of returning to Richmond a wealthy man, he was robbed and murdered.

Founder of Modern Orthopaedics

Richmond is the birthplace of medical pioneer Dr Emil Hoffa. Once a pupil of Helena Gilstain, Hoffa is hailed as the founder of modern orthopaedics. Born in Richmond on March 31, 1859, son of a local doctor, he studied medicine in Germany, and in 1886 became a lecturer at the University of Wuerzburg. He later became a Professor and moved to Berlin. Dr Hoffa died in December, 1907: many of his textbooks and techniques are still in use.

In keeping with this Karoo tradition of producing great medical people, heart transplant pioneer Professor Chris Barnard spends a great deal of time at his Richmond farm, Ratelfontein.

The Village Soldiers On

By 1866, Richmond had grown so rapidly that the first bank was established, this despite the Karoo being in the grips of drought and a failing economy. By 1867, the entire Cape Colony was virtually bankrupt. The causes were severe droughts and the Basuto Wars. Several towns in the Cape and Northern Karoo had helped Free Staters in these conflicts.

Bid for Overseas Trade

Early in 1867, Governor Philip Wodehouse tried to improve the economy of the Colony by promoting overseas trade. A committee then secured exhibits for the huge Paris International Exhibition of 1867.

A Richmond farmer set the example in the Karoo by submitting examples of wheat, barley, sheep and ox tallow, sheep tail fat, oil, beeswax, ganna ash (invaluable in soap making) and one bar of Boer soap. These were among items from the interior first shown in Cape Town before being shipped to Paris. Both local and international exhibitions were successful, and the products were highly acclaimed. But Cape people were enraged when they heard that the Paris exhibition judges had drunk 60 bottles of Cape wine and eaten all the Karoo preserves.

A Newspaper Appears

With progress came the launching in 1870 of a local newspaper, now long gone. With the bold title of The Era, it reported on happenings in the town and district, and enjoyed wide popularity. On July 20, 1876, The Era carried a story recording the opening of a new public school. It was then that Helena Gilstain took her talents to a farm school. Years later, The Era also extensively covered the Boer War. Among the stories was one telling of a badly wounded Boer leader, Commandant Smit, being sped away by horse and cart to a doctor at Murraysburg.

Boer War Attacks

During the Anglo-Boer War the town was twice attacked by the Boers. Several graves in the old Dutch Reformed Cemetery, as well as in the tiny, overgrown Anglican cemetery, serve as reminders. As with most South African towns of the time, Richmond had both British and Boer supporters, but it was difficult for Boer sympathisers to openly display feelings as martial law had been imposed throughout the Cape Colony from December, 1900.

Deelfontein - Paradox of the Plains

It's only a lonely little railway siding on the plains of the Great Karoo, but what makes Deelfontein eerily different are its buildings and the neat rows of graves nearby. The

dilapidated buildings hint at a Victorian elegance, but they came a little late to share in that chapter of history. The Yeomanry Hotel was built to accommodate the grieving relatives of those who died at this once huge military hospital. In its time it was the largest surgical and convalescent hospital in the Colony. It also had an X-ray installation, probably among the first to be used in a military hospital. There are two cemeteries at Deelfontein, a small one with five graves and the larger with 134. Almost all soldiers buried here died of typhoid.

Rich Architectural Styles

The first impression of Richmond and its buildings is that of a restful, historical and quaint country town, a charming example of mid-19th century Karoo architecture. Many of the houses were built before 1890, but their age is often difficult to judge because verandas and pillars were subsequently added. Most of these additions date back to the 1920s. While the congregation dates back to 1843, the church was only inaugurated in 1847. This imposing building was later enlarged and a tower was added in 1909. The pulpit, said to be the tallest in the country, was carved by L. F. Anhuyse in 1854, who did similar work for the Groote Kerk in Cape Town.

Ancient Footprints, A Ship's Mast and Hunting

There are several interesting farms in the district. On Klipplaat there are 60 claw-like fossilised footprints. These are believed to have been made by an Aulacephalodon, a slow-moving, plant-eating reptile that roamed these plains about 250-million years ago. And on Ouplaas there is an old horse-driven flour mill which is still in working order. The axle, once a ship's mast, reaches from the floor to the yellow wood attic. The nameplate on the hopper states this mill was built by Charles Bridger, a well-known millwright of his day.

Bird watching, game viewing and springbok hunting are popular.

KAROO RICHMOND, CAPE PROVINCE

Karoo town situated in the Bo-Karoo next to the N1 approximately halfway between Cape Town and Gauteng. It is a quaint town with lots of trees. Due to the high altitude, summers are pleasant and not quite as hot as one would expect from a Karoo town. Winters do however have some very cold spells with frost and in some years, snow.

It is a farming town which is now also known as Richmond Booktown, with a newly established annual Book Festival in October.

There is an old age home, hospital , doctor, two small supermarkets, butchery specialising in venison, various small businesses, bottle stores, co-op, service station, country club with golf course, saddle horse museum, library, municipal office, prison, police station, magistrate's court, post office, traffic department, various restaurants, bed and bed breakfast establishments, churches, bookshops, gallery and school.

A local monthly newsletter is published and can be accessed via the richmondnc.co.za web page under the heading Richmondnuus. *(Source: www. richmondnc.co.za)*

RICHMOND, KWAZULU-NATAL

Richmond is a town situated on the banks of the upper Illovo River in the midlands of KwaZulu-Natal, South Africa, approximately 38 km south-west of Pietermaritzburg.

History

Richmond was established in 1850 as Beaulieu-on-Illovo by British Byrne Settlers who were originally from Beaulieu, the seat of the Duke of Buccleuch in Richmond, North Yorkshire. The name was later changed to Richmond for ease of pronunciation.

The arrival of the settlers brought about a slow return of various remnants of African people who fled the raiding Zulu armies. The Zulus called these refugees "amaBhaca", (people who hide). Although composed of elements of many different groups, the Bhaca have developed their own identity.

In February 1906 two British officers were killed at Byrne, near Richmond while involved in enforcing the collection of the hated Poll Tax from "recalcitrant districts". This incident, known as the 'Trewirgie Incident', precipitated the imposition of martial law and set off the Bambatha Rebellion.

One of Natal's greatest tycoons, Joseph Baynes, a Yorkshireman by birth, was a pioneer of the dairy industry. His Baynesfield Estate was bequeathed in his will to the nation of South Africa.

Timber, sugarcane, poultry, citrus fruit and dairy goods are produced here. The town is located within the Richmond Municipality, forming part of the Umgungundlovu District Municipality and incorporates the former township of Ndaleni on the opposite bank of the Illovo River.

RICHMONDS: CARIBBEAN

Jamaica is an island country and is the third-largest island of the Greater Antilles. The island is south of Cuba and West of Hispaniola; it contains the nation-states of Haiti and the Dominican Republic. Jamaica is the fifth-largest island country in the Caribbean.

History

The indigenous people are the Taino who called it the "Land of Wood and Water" or the "Land of Springs" Its population is estimated at 2.8million.

Once a Spanish possession known as *Santiago*, in 1655 it came under the rule of England (later Great Britain), and was called Jamaica. It achieved full independence from the United Kingdom on August 6, 1962. With 2.8 million people, it is the third most populous Anglophone country in the Americas, after the United States and Canada.

Kingston is the country's largest city, with a population of 937,700, and its capital. Jamaica has a large diaspora around the world consisting of Jamaican citizens migrating from the country.

Music

Though a small nation, Jamaican culture has a strong global presence. The musical genres reggae, ska mento, rock steady club, and, more recently, dancehall and ragga all originated in the island's vibrant, popular urban recording industry. Jamaica also played an important role in the development of punk rock through reggae and ska. Reggae has also influenced American rap music, as they both share their roots as rhythmic, African styles of music. Some rappers, such as The Notorius B.I.G and HeavyD, are of Jamaican descent. Internationally known reggae musician Bob Marley was also Jamaican.

Many other internationally known artists were born in Jamaica including Millie Small, Lee Scratch Perry, Peter Tosh, Jimmy Cliff, Grace Jones and many more artists. Genre jungle emerged from London's Jamaican diaspora. The birth of hip-hop in New York City, New York also owed much to the city's Jamaican community.

Ian Fleming, who lived in Jamaica, repeatedly used the island as a setting in the James Bond novels, including 'Live and Let Die'; 'Doctor No'; 'For Your Eyes Only'; 'The Man with Golden Gun'; 'Octopussy' and 'The Living Daylights'. James Bond uses a Jamaica-based cover in 'Casino Royale'. So far, the only James Bond film adaptation to have been set in Jamaica is 'Doctor No'. Filming for the fictional island of San Monique in 'Live and Let Die' took place in Jamaica.

Blue Mountains Jamaica, permission of Jamacian tourist board.

RICHMOND, PARISH OF ST MARYS, JAMAICA

This was originally an estate owned by a family named "Meek" and was called "Meek Spring". The Meek's sold it to the Duke of Richmond whence it's name.

[There are reportedly four Richmonds in Jamaica - Richmond Hill, Richmond Crescent and Richmond Drive as well as the one above. I rang Jamaican Tourist Board in London in February 2013 and they confirmed this. BS]

GRENADA

Grenada is also known as the "Island of Spice" because of the production of nutmeg crops of which Grenada is one of the world's largest exporters. Its size is 344 square kilometres (133 sq miles), with an estimated population of 110,000. Its capital is St Georges. The National Bird of Grenada is the critically endangered Grenada Dove.

(Kind permission of Grenada Tourist Board)

Richmond, Granville Bay

A small settlement.

RICHMOND HILL, ST GEORGES

A much larger settlement near the capital. *(Source: Grenada Tourist Board, London, April 2013).*

TOBAGO

Tobago has a land area of 300 kilometres; approximately 42 kilometres long by 10 kilometres wide and is slightly north of Trinidad. In 2011 (Census) the population was 60,874.

Its capital Scarborough is named after North Yorkshire town (the first Victorian Spa town in the world) and has a population of about 17,000

While Trinidad is multi-ethnic, the population of Tobago is primarily of African descent, although with a growing proportion of Trinidadians of East Indian descent and Europeans (predominantly Germans and Scandinavians). Between 2000 and 2011, the population of Tobago grew by 12.55 percent, making it one of the fastest growing areas of the country.

Tobago is primarily hilly and of volcanic origin: the south-west of the island is flat and consists largely of coral limestone; the hilly spine of the island is known as Main Ridge. Its highest point is the 550 metre (1804 feet) Pigeon Peak near Speyside.

Tobago is divided into seven parishes – three in the Western Region and four in the Eastern Region. *(Kind permission of Tobago Tourist Board)*

It features two Richmonds:

Richmond Great House Hotel and a small island off the coast called **Richmond Island**.

MONTSERRAT

Montserrat is a Caribbean island that is a British Overseas Territory. It is located in the Leeward Islands, part of the chain of islands known as the Lesser Antilles, in the West Indies. The island of Montserrat measures approximately 16 kilometers (9.9 miles) long by 11 kilometers (6.8 miles) wide, with approximately 40 kilometers (25 miles) of coastline.

Montserrat is nicknamed *The Emerald Isle of the Caribbean* both for its resemblance to coastal Ireland and for the Irish ancestry of some of its inhabitants. Richmond Hill is on west side of island

On 18 July 1995, the previously dormant Soufriere Hills Volcano became active. Eruptions destroyed Montserrat's Georgian-era capital city of Plymouth and two-thirds of the island's population was forced to flee. The volcanic activity continues to the present, the affected areas currently being mostly in the vicinity of Plymouth, including its docking facilities, and also on the Eastern side of the island in the area around the former W.H. Bramble named after chief minister stopped being in use 1997 and the remnants of which were buried by flows from volcanic activity on 11 February 2010.

An "exclusion zone" extending from the South coast of the island North to parts of the Belham Valley has been imposed because of the size of the existing volcanic dome and the resulting potential for pyroclastic activity and volcanic lava flow.

RICHMOND, VERMONT, CHITTENDEN COUNTY

In 1775, Amos Brownson and John Chamberlain made the first settlement attempt. They abandoned their efforts in the fall of that year, but returned in the spring of 1784, at the close of the Revolutionary War. Richmond was incorporated by the General Assembly on October 27, 1794, and then organized in 1795. The Winooski River and Huntington River both offered locations for water mills. Industries began to manufacture wagons, harnesses, tinware, brass, cabinet work and wooden-ware. By 1859, the population was 1,453.

Richmond is noted for the Round Church; a rare 16-sided meetinghouse that was erected in 1812-1813.

RICHMOND HILL, EXUMA, BAHAMAS

Richmond Hill is an attractive settlement on these islands which has not been lived in for 10 years. No doubt someone may well live there again

History

The Exumas are the historic home of the Lucan natives, who were wholly enslaved in the 16th century, leaving the islands uninhabited until the 18th century. In the intervening period, the Exumas provided many hideouts and stashes for pirates: Elizabeth Harbor was a favorite lair of Captain Kidd.

Exuma was settled in or around 1783 by American loyalists fleeing the Revolutionary War. The expatriates brought a cotton plantation economy to the islands. George Town was named in honor of George III, to whom the settlers maintained their loyalty.

The capital and largest city in the district is George Town (permanent population 1,000), founded 1793 and located on Great Exuma.

John Rolle, First Baron Rolle, a major Loyalist settler of the Exumas, is a major figure in the islands' heritage. Upon his death in 1842, he bestowed all of his significant Exuma land

holdings to his slaves. As a result, a number of towns on Great Exuma have been named after him such as Rolleville and Rolletown.

Between 2000 and 2010, the population of Exuma more than doubled, reflecting the construction of large and small resort properties and the related increased direct airlift to Great Exuma from locations as distant as Toronto, Canada.

Geography

Exuma is a district of the Bahamas, consisting of over 360 islands or Cays. The largest of the Cays is Great Exuma, which is 37 miles (60 kilometers) in length and joined to another island, Little Exuma by a small bridge. The Tropic of Cancer runs across a beach close to the city. The entire island chain is 130 miles (209 kilometers) long and 27 square miles (72 kilometers^2) in area.

A few smaller Cays still remain grandfathered as partially or wholly private, (still referred to as part of the Exuma-Bahamas Cays) and located by a three digit suffix number (ex. Exuma xxx). Most noted are Exuma 642, and 643 which in recent years have had their life-spans shortened by receding shorelines.

Attractions

- The islands are a popular spot for yachting sailing diving, and coral reef and cave exploring.
- Many of the unnamed beaches and coves of the islands, including extensive offshore reef areas, are included in the protected Exuma National Land and Sea Park of the Bahamas National Trust.
- Some of the islands on which there are permanent residents and resorts include Staniel Cay Staniel Cay (home of the Staniel Cay Yacht Club, a fixture in the Exumas), Fowl Cay, Musha Cay and Iguana Cay.

- Thunderball Grotto, located just a few hundred yards off Staniel Cay, is one location where the James Bond's 'Thunderball' was filmed.
- Sandy Cay, just a short boat ride from Little Exuma was the location used for filming the 'Pirates of the Caribbean' beach scenes and one Shell commercial.
- The novel Wind from Carolinas was set in Great Exuma.
- Wild Swimming pigs of Pig Island Exuma love swimming in the Bahamas

Notable residents

The main island has been a haven for celebrities for years. Until recently, the tourist population on the island was extremely minimal, allowing anonymity for anyone escaping the spotlight. Frequent visitors included:

- Princess Margaret, Countess of Snowdon, who stayed at Goat Cay (the home of Babbie Holt)
- Jackie Onassis
- Jessica Tandy and Hume Cronin; the married couple spent a lot of time on the island also at Goat Cay for many years, and Sigourney Weaver vacationed there with her family.

In light of the relatively low cost of purchasing islands and the relatively low Bahamian tax regime for non-locals, a number of celebrities own islands in the Exumas. These include:

- Aga Khan
- Nicholas Cage
- David Copperfield
- Ali Daei
- Johnny Depp
- Faith Hill and Tim Mcgraw
- Ali Karimi
- Eddie Murphy
- Edie Irvine

Transportation

Exuma International Airport serves the city of George Town directly from Nassau Miami, Atlanta and Toronto. Staniel Cay also has a small airstrip.

Acklins and Crooked Islands Bahamas

Acklins and Crooked Islands was a district of the Bahamas until 1996 and as Acklins, Crooked Island and Long Cay until 1999.

There is meant to be Richmond City on Acklin Island [*but this is, as yet, unconfirmed*].

History

The islands were settled by American Loyalists in the late 1780s who set cotton plantations employing over 1,000 slaves. After the abolition of slavery in the British Empire these became uneconomical, and the replacement income from sponge diving has now dwindled as well. The inhabitants now live by fishing and small-scale farming.

The main town in the group is Colonel Hill on Crooked Island. Albert Town, on Long Cay, now sparsely populated, was once a prosperous little town. It was engaged in the sponge and salt industries and also served as a transfer port for stevedores seeking work on passing ships. The population of Acklins was 428, and Crooked Island 350, at the 2000 census.

Since 1999, Acklins and Crooked Island are separate districts.

Geography

These consist of a group of islands semi-encircling a large, shallow Lagoon called the Bight of Acklins, of which the largest are Crooked Island in the North and Acklins in the South-east; the smaller are Long Cay (once known as Fortune Island) in the North-west, and Castle Island in the South.

RICHMOND, BEQUIA, GRENADINES

This is a small island, measuring 7 square miles (18 km²) with a population of approximately 4,300. The native population is primarily a mixture of people of African Scottish and Carib Indian descent. A substantial number of white Barbadians also settled the Mount Pleasant area of Bequia in the 1860s. Many of their descendants still inhabit the area. Other highly populated areas include the island capital, Port Elizabeth, which hosts the ferry terminal and Paget Farm, which hosts the airport. There are also villages at Lower Bay, La Pompe, Hamilton and Belmont. Other prominent areas of Bequia include Spring, the site of a former coconut plantation and home to agricultural animals, Industry Bay and Park Bay, where the Old Hegg Turtle Sanctuary is located.

Princess Margaret, who had a home on nearby Mustique, visited Bequia and had a beach named in her honour. *Princess Margaret Beach* is next to Port Elizabeth and is situated inside Admiralty Bay on the west coast. Also on the west coast are the island's main port and a large natural harbour/port in Bequia. The opening shot of the movie Blackbeard pirate of Caribbean, made by the BBC, displays a replica of his first ship off the coast of Bequia in the St. Vincent passage. According to local legend, Saint Vincent and the Grenadines was not only Captain Edward Teach's base, but also the place from which Sir Francis Drake planned his attacks on the Spanish admiralty in Don Blas de Lezos's Cartagena. Indeed, it is thought that Henry Morgan may also have anchored in Admiralty Bay as it was then the safest natural harbour in the Eastern Caribbean during hurricane season. Bequia is one of the few places in the world where limited whaling is still allowed by the international whaling commission. Natives of Bequia are allowed to catch up to four humpback whales per year using only traditional hunting methods of hand-thrown harpoons in small, open sailboats. Richmond is beautiful situated on west coast be about 50 homes and near to capital Port Elizabeth.

RICHMOND, ST VINCENT

Richmond is small settlement on the island and Richmond River is very close. Richmond Peak (1075 metres) looks over the settlement.

Saint Vincent is a volcanic island in the Caribbean. It is the largest island of the country and is located in the Caribbean Sea, between Saint Lucia and Grenada. It is composed of partially submerged volcanic mountains. Its largest volcano and highest peak of the country, La Soufriere is active having last erupted in 1979.

The territory was disputed between France and the UK in the 18th century, before being ceded to the British in 1763 and again in 1783. It gained independence on October 27, 1979. Approximately 100,000 people live on the island. Kingston, (population 25,418) is the chief town. The rest of the population is dispersed along the coastal strip, which includes the other five main towns of Layoub, Barrouille, Chateaublair, George Town and Calliaqua.

RICHMONDS: SRI LANKA

RICHMOND, CASTLE GALLE

Galle is the administrative capital of Southern province with a population of 98,000 and the fifth largest city in the country, after the capital Colombo.

History

Before the arrival of the Portuguese in the 16th century, it was the main port on the island. Galle reached the height of its development in the 18th century, during the Dutch colonial period. It is the best example of a fortified city built by the Portuguese in South and Southeast Asia. The Galle fortress a World Heritage Site and is the largest remaining Fortress in Asia built by European occupiers.

Richmond Castle (located in Palathota, close Kaluthara town, Western province of Sri Lanka) was built by Arthur de Silva Wijeyasing Padikara Mudali (1889-1947), but he didn't stay in this place in the last days of his life. It is currently is placing used as a Children Orphanage and community activities of the area.

This mansion is famous for its remarkable architectural features and one of the few remaining buildings belonging to that era.

On 26 December 2004, the city was devastated by the massive boxing day Tsunami caused by the 2004 Indian Ocean earthquake that occurred a thousand miles away, off the coast of Indonesia. Thousands were killed in the city alone.

Galle is home to a cricket ground, the Galle International stadium, rebuilt after the tsunami. Test matches resumed there on December 18, 2007.

(By kind permission of Sri Lanka High Commission 2013)

Richmond College is a primary and secondary school in Galle Sri Lanka. The school was started as a Galle High School in 1876 by Reverend George Baugh and is now a well-established institution with a reputation as one of the finest schools in Sri Lanka.

Approaching the end of its second century as a school, it has produced many prominent citizens, including two in the highest political positions, namely the current President, and a former Prime Minister.

Richmond College Union, UK

The Old Boys Association was named as Richmond College Union in the UK as a new concept; a new constitution was drafted and accepted by the membership. The aims and objectives of the Union were to assist the College and its pupils to further the welfare and in the advancement of the education by providing any form of assistance as appropriate. In addition, the Union would foster camaraderie and brotherhood amongst the expatriate old boys (and girls) living in UK. Any past pupil or teacher of the College and interested in actively furthering the Objectives of the association would be eligible to be a member. From the small beginnings, the Union continued to flourish from strength to strength. More members were enrolled; regular contributions were made to the College for purchase of sporting equipment, books and various other major needs.

At the 2nd Annual General Meeting, Lionel Goonatillake was elected as the secretary and Dr Jeewa Siriwardena as the president. The 1st dinner/Dance Richmond Nite was held in November 1991. Since then this event has become a regular social event creating a wonderful atmosphere for the families of the members and their friends to get together. It also has raised significant funds, which have been donated to the College for educational and sporting developments.

By kind permission of Sri Lanka Tourist Promotion Board 2013.

RICHMONDS: FIJI

RICHMOND HILL, KADAVU ISLAND

Richmond is small settlement on Island of Kavadu, in an idyllic setting and less developed than other islands.

History

In the 17th and 18th centuries the Dutch and British explored Fiji, which became a British colony until 1970, British administration having lasted almost a century. During World War II, thousands of Fijians volunteered to aid in Allied efforts via their attachment to the New Zealand and Australian army units. The Republic of Fiji Military Forces (RFMF) consist of land and naval units.

Fiji is one of the most developed economies in the Pacific Island realm due to an abundance of forest, mineral and fish resources. Today, the main sources of foreign exchange are its tourist industry and sugar exports. The country's currency is the Fijian Dollar.

Following a Coup in 2006, Ratu Epeli Nailatikau became Fiji's president after a high court ruled that the military leadership was unlawfully appointed. Fiji's local government, in the form of city and town councils, is supervised by the Ministry of Local Government and Urban Development.

Geography

The Republic of Fiji is an island country in Melanasia in the South Pacific Ocean about 1,100 nautical miles Northeast of New Zealand North Island. Its closest neighbours are Vanuatu to the west, Frances New Caledonia to the Southwest, New Zealand's Kermadec to the southeast, Tonga to the east, the Samoas, France's Wallis and Futuma to the Northeast and Tuvalu to the North.

The majority of Fiji's islands were formed through volcanic activity starting around 150 million years ago. Today, some geothermal activity still occurs on the islands of Vanua Levu and Taveuni. Fiji has been inhabited since the second millennium BC. The country comprises an archipelago of more than 332 islands, of which 110 are permanently inhabited, and more than 500 islets, amounting to a total land area of circa 7,100 square miles. The two major islands, Vitii and Vanua Levu account for 87% of the population of almost 850,000. The former contains Suva, the capital and largest city. Most Fijians live on Viti Levu's coasts, either in Suva or in smaller urban centres. Viti Levu's interior is sparsely inhabited due to its terrain. Richmond Hill is on Kavadu Island

Sport

Rugby Union is the most-popular team sport played in Fiji. The national rugby union team is very successful given the size of the population of the country, and has competed at five Rugby World Cup competitions, the first being in 1987, where they reached the quarter-finals. The Fiji national side did not match that feat again until the Rugby World Cup in 2007 when they upset Wales 38–34 to progress to the quarter-finals where they nearly beat the eventual Rugby World Cup winners, South Africa. Fiji also defeated the British and Irish Lions in 1977. Fiji competes in the Pacific Tri Nations and the IRB Pacific Nations Cup. The sport is governed by the Fiji Rugby Union which is a member of the Pacific islands rugby alliance, and contributes to the Pacific Islanders rugby union team. At the club level there are the Colonial Cup and Pacific Rugby Cup. The Fijian sevens team is one of the most successful rugby sevens teams in the world, having won two world cup titles and the 2006 IRB Series and playing very well in IRB Sevens 2012/13 Season.

The Fiji national rugby union team is a member of the Pacific Islands Rugby Alliance (PIRA) formerly along with Samoa and Tonga. In 2009, Samoa announced their departure from the Pacific Islands Rugby Alliance, leaving just Fiji and Tonga in the union. Fiji is currently ranked sixteenth in the world by the IRB (as of 26 September 2011). Despite this low rating, in the 2007 Rugby World Cup Fiji defeated Wales 38–34 to claim a quarter final spot (theoretically placing them in the top 8 teams in the world) and proceeded to give eventual winners South Africa a scare eventually going down 37–20.

Fiji is one of the few countries where rugby is the main sport. There are approximately 80,000 registered players from a total population of around 950,000. One of the problems for Fiji is simply getting their players to play for their home country, as many have contracts in Europe or with Super

Rugby teams, where monetary compensation is far more rewarding. The repatriated salaries of its overseas stars have become an important part of some local economies. In addition, a significant number of players eligible to play for Fiji end up representing Australia or New Zealand; notable examples are Fiji-born cousins and current new Zealand All Blacks, Joe Rokocoko and Sitiveni Sivivatu and as well as Australian Wallabies Winger, Lote Tuqiri. Fiji has won the most Pacific Tri-Nations Championships of the three participating teams.

RICHMOND HIGH SCHOOL, KADAVU ISLAND

RICHMONDS: INDIA

RICHMOND, BANGALORE, STATE OF KAMATAKA

Richmond is small suburb in Bangalore, which is the capital of the State of Kamataka, as well as being India's third most populous city with an estimated 8m residents. Bangalore is well- known as a hub for India's information technology sector and is among the top 10 preferred entrepreneurial locations in the world. As a growing metropolitan city in a developing country, Bangalore confronts substantial pollution and other logistical and socio-economic problems.

A succession of South Indian dynasties ruled the region of Bangalore until in 1537, Kempe Govda feudatory ruler under the Vijavanagara. Following the independence from Great Britain in 1947, Bangalore became the capital of Mysore State and remained capital when the new Indian state of Karnataka was formed in 1956. With a GDP of $83 billion, Bangalore is listed 4th among the top 15 cities contributing to India's overall GDP.

Richmond Bangalore .

COMMONWEALTH OF NATIONS

This is normally referred to as **The Commonwealth** and formerly known as the **British Commonwealth**. It is an inter-governmental organisation of 54 independent member states. All members except Mozambique and Rwanda and were part of the British Empire out of which the Commonwealth developed to present.

The member states cooperate within a framework of common values and goals, as outlined in the Singapore Declaration. These include the promotion of democracy, human rights, good governance, the rule of law, individual liberty, egalitarianism, free trade, multi- lateralism, and world peace.

The Commonwealth is not a political union, but an intergovernmental organisation in which countries with diverse social, political and economic backgrounds are regarded as equal in status. Alongside shared values, Commonwealth nations share strong trade links; trade with another Commonwealth member has been shown to be a third to a half more than with a non-member.

Activities of the Commonwealth are carried out through the permanent Commonwealth, headed by the secretary general and biennial meetings of Commonwealth heads. The symbol of their free association is the Head of the Commonwealth, currently held by Queen Elizabeth II. Elizabeth II is also monarch, separately and independently, of 16 Commonwealth members, which are known as the Commonwealth Realms.

The Commonwealth is a forum for a number of non-governmental organisations, collectively known as the Commonwealth Family, which are fostered through the inter-governmental Commonwealth Foundation. The Commonwealth Games, the Commonwealth's most visible activity, are a product of one of these organisations and is to be held in august 2014 Glasgow and Edinburgh. These organisations strengthen the shared culture of the Commonwealth, which extends through common sports, literary heritage, and political and legal practices. Reflecting this, diplomatic missions between Commonwealth countries are designated as High Commissions rather than Embassies. *(Source: Wikipedia)*

NOTABLE PEOPLE, RICHMOND, NORTH YORKSHIRE

This is not a definitive list.

Notable inhabitants

Born in Richmond

Rob Andrew: Rugby Union International

Christopher Craddock: Rear Admiral

George Cuitt: Painter

John James Fenwick: founder of Fenwick's department stores

Henry Greathead: Inventor of the lifeboat

Brenda Hale: Baroness Hale of Richmond, a Justice of the Supreme Court of UK

Joanne Jackson: Olympic swimmer

Herbert Sedwick: First class cricketer

Theo Hutcraft: One half of synth-pop duo, Hurts

Oliver Catt: Musician and principal member of Fantasy Rainbow

Francis Johnson: Dissenter

John Lawrence: 1st Baron Lawrence, Viceroy of India

Amanda Berry CEO of BAFTA

Tim Rodber: Rugby union international.

Edward Roper: First class cricketer

James Tate: (11 June 1771-1843) Headmaster of Richmond School. He was appointed on 27 September 1796, the fulfillment of a childhood ambition. Tate was responsible for transforming the school into one of the leading classical schools of its day, and the leading Whig school, attracting boys from throughout the country, at a rate of 100 guineas a year. Between 1812 and 1833 six pupils a year on average proceeded to university. 21 of them became fellows 13 of them at Trinity College Cambridge. They became so "successful, admired and feared" whilst at Cambridge that they earned the title of 'Tate's Invincibles'.

Thomas Taylor: Clergyman. Taylor was born in 1576 in Richmond where his father was known as a friend to Puritans and silenced ministers in the North. He distinguished himself at Cambridge, became a fellow and reader in Hebrew at Christ's College, gained Bachelor of Divinity 1628, and was incorporated Doctor of Divinity at Oxford in 1630. He began preaching at 21 and when only about 25 when he preached a sermon at St Paul's Cross before Queen Elizabeth I. He was known for strong anti-Roman Catholic views.

Notable residents

Robert Barclay Allardice: pedestrian, educated at Richmond School. He was universally known as Captain Barclay and born in August 1777 at Ury House just outside Stonehaven in Scotland. Barclay was one of the strongest men of his time, which seems to have been a family trait. His family were famous for their muscular prowess and pastimes such as wrestling bulls, carrying sacks of flour in their teeth and uprooting trees with their bare hands were part of the Barclay family tradition. As a boy, Barclay played with a two-handed sword which was too heavy for most grown men to lift.

By the age of 20, he could lift an 18 stone man from the floor to a table with one hand. Hammer throwing and caber tossing were like children's games to him.

John Bathurst: Physician to Oliver Cromwell. The family built The Kings Head Hotel, Richmond and the Colonel Bathurst Inn, Reeth (licensed to marry walkers).

Marcus Beresford: Primate of Ireland.

Lewis Carroll: Author, attended Richmond School,

John Butler Clark: Historian of Spain.

J R Cohu: Headmaster of Richmond School.

Edward Ellerton: Educational philanthropist, educated at Richmond School.

Charles Grey: 2nd Earl of Grey, British Prime Minister. Educated at Richmond School.

Angela Harris: Baroness Harris of Richmond, Deputy Speaker in the House of Lords.

Thomas Hounsfield: First class cricketer.

Samuel Howit: Painter.

Peter Inge: Baron Inge, head of the British Army.

Philip Mayne: Last surviving British officer of the First World War. No

George Peacock: Mathematician, attended a school in Richmond; one of "Tate's Invincibles".

Donald Peers: Singer.

James Raine: Antiquarian, educated at Richmond School, one of "Tate's Invincibles"

Thomas Sedgwick (Segiswycke): died 1573 in a Yorkshire prison. An English Roman Catholic theologian. An unfriendly hand in 1562 describes him as "learned but not very wise". He was restricted to within ten miles of Richmond Yorkshire, from 1562 to 1570, when he seems to have been sent to prison at York.

Richard Sheepshanks: Astronomer. Educated at Richmond School, one of "Tate's Invincibles".

RICHMOND OF THE WORLD 2013 EVENTS

Many of the events featured here run annually. Please check all events for accuracy.

JANUARY 2013
26 Australia Day

FEBRUARY 2013
Annual Crab Feed Day Richmond, California
Richmond Nelson Summer Fayre
Richmond Arts Festival, Melbourne
Presidents Day USA (18)
Richmond Hill Winter Festival, Ontario (1-3)
Richmond Sri Lanka Elephant Polo Tournament
Farmers Cay Festival Richmond, Bahamas

MARCH 2013
Second Tuesday in March, Commonwealth Day
Freeport Richmond, Bahamas
Bacardi Billfish Tournament, Bahamas
Richmond Village Colonial Fair, Tasmania

APRIL 2013
Goat and Crab Race Richmond, Tobago (9/10)
Cricket: Richmond, Yorkshire v Richmond, London return match from Sept 15 2012 (13/14)
97th Black and White Show Holstein Cattle, Richmond, Utah
Historic Richmond Town, New York BBQ Cook-off (20)
St Georges Day, UK (23)
Tobago Jazz Experience (TJE) (20-28)
Bahamas Family Island Regatta Richmond Hill, Exumas

MAY 2013
Richmond Meet, Yorkshire (27-30)
Richmond May Fair, London (11)
Mad Hatters Tea Party Richmond, NSW
Richmond Fossil Festival may 2014 Queensland –
Earth Day Richmond Rhode Island, US
Battle of Richmond Tours, Kentucky (May-Sept)
Richmond, Vancouver Delta Regional Heritage Show (13/14)
Richmond Cruise Nights, Illinois (May-June)
Richmond's Summer Night Market & Richmond Night Market (May and Oct) Vancouver

JUNE 2013

Heritage Village Festival Richmond Hill, Ontario
Harness Racing Richmond, Nelson, NZ
Richmond Day, Part of Swaledale Festival Yorkshire (4)
New Richmond Bluegrass Festival, Quebec (24)

JULY 2013

Canada Day (1)
American Independence Day (4)
Rabbit Island Triathlon, Richmond, Nelson NZ
Heart of Minnesota Fish Tournament
Stevenson Salmon Festival Richmond, British Colombia (1)
Stampede Richmond, Calgary, Canada (5-14)
Richmond Days Maine, US (26 /27)

AUGUST 2013

Richmond County Show Virginia, US (21/22)
Richmond Live, Yorkshire (2-3)
Richmond Riverside Festival, London
Richmond Jazz Festival, Virginia US
Richmond Open Summer Markets Richmond, British Colombia
Jamaica Independence Day (6)

SEPTEMBER 2013

Richmond Walk and Fame Michigan, US
Richmond Fair Ottawa
Richmond County Agricultural Show, North Carolina
Richmond Good Old Days Richmond, Michigan (5-8)
Great River Race Richmond, London (7)
ROW Convention Richmond, London (7)
Richmond Walking and Book Festival, Yorkshire (Sept /Oct)
225th birthday of The Georgian Theatre Royal, Yorkshire (9)
Richmond Heart Walk, (21) Virginia

OCTOBER 2013

Festival of Lights Richmond, Fiji
Great Ogeechee Seafood Festival Richmond Hill, Georgia
Fiji Day Trinidad and Tobago (10)
Richmond Folk Festival, Virginia (11-13)
Columbus Day US (14)
Golden Hills Marathon Richmond, CA Berkeley (21)
Pumpkin Picking Decker Farm Richmond, Staten Island

NOVEMBER 2013

Bonfire Night, Worldwide (5)

White Water Rafting Richmond, Natal, South Africa

Richmond, London, Literary Festival (All Nov)

Artisan and Antiques Fair Richmond, Texas

Cranberry and Slugfest Richmond, Vancouver

Thanksgiving Day, USA (28)

Ladies Polo and Hector Smith Trophy, Richmond, NSW (11)

Taste the Local West Broad Village Festival, Richmond, Virginia

Richmond Cider Week Richmond, Virginia

Montserrat Volcano Half Marathon – Montserrat

DECEMBER 2013

Richmond Market Day, Nelson, NZ

Kris Kringle Day, Minnesota (10)

Junkanoo Boxing Day Festival Richmond, Bahamas (26)

2014

ROW Golf Tournament, Yorkshire August 1 (Yorkshire Day)

90 TH YEAR OF RICHMOND LONDON ROTARY

Commonwealth Games Edinburgh and Glasgow: there are 20 Richmonds in the Commonwealth

2015

WORLD CYCLING CHAMPIONSHION, Virginia

'Richmonds of World' Convention, Virginia.

If you have any ideas and events to include or any comments, please send to: richmondsoftheworld@gmail.com

RICHMONDS OF THE WORLD WEBSITES –

Here are most of web site addresses from the list above:

www.richmond.org	North Yorkshire
www.visitrichmond.com	London
www.visitrichmondva.com	Virginia
www.richmondgresthouse.com	Tobago
www.richmond-utah.com	Utah
www.richmondmaine.com	Maine
www.richmondma.org	Massachusetts
www.ci.richmond.ca.us OR www.richmondvillage.ca.us	California
www.richmond-il.com	Illinois
www.richmond.ky.us	Kentucky
www.cityofrichmond.net	Michigan
www.cityofrichmondmo.org	Missouri
www.historicrichmond.org	Staten Island
www.keene.h.com	New Hampshire
www.richmondri.com	Rhode Island
www.richmond.tx.nww.net	Texas
www. richmondvt.com	Vermont
www.newrichmondwi.gov	Wisconsin
www.richmond.ca	Vancouver
www.richmond village.com.au	Tasmania
www.about.nsw.gov.au	New South Wales
www.richmond.qld.gov.au	Queensland
www.richmondcollege.lk	Sri Lanka
www.fijime.com	Fiji
www.bequiatourism.com	Bequia
www.exumabahamas.com	Bahamas
www.visitmelbourne.com	Melbourne
www.visitcalgary.com	Calgary
www.richmondcounty.ca	Novia Scotia
www.yorkshiredales.org	Yorkshire Dales
www.swaledale.org	Yorkshire Dales

This was kindly compiled by Rick Tatnall, Virginia 2012, who is very keen to see the development of the Richmonds of the World concept.

PLACE			
Richmond	New South Wales	City of Hawkesbury	Town
Richmond	Queensland		Town
Richmond	South Australia	City of West Torrens	Suburb
Richmond	Tasmania	Hobart	Town
Richmond	Victoria	Melbourne	Suburb
New Richmond	Quebec	Municipality	Unincorporated
Richmond	Alberta	Calgary	Neighborhood
Richmond	British Columbia	City of Richmond	
Richmond	Ontario	Elgin County	Village
Richmond County	Nova Scotia		
Richmond	Prince Edward Island	Municipality	Incorporated
Richmond	Quebec		Town
Richmond Corner	New Brunswick	Woodstock	Neighborhood
Richmond Heights	Saskatchewan	City of Saskatoon	Neighborhood
Richmond Hill	Ontario	Greater Toronto	Town
Richmond	Fiji	Kadavu Island	Town
Richmond Town	India	City of Bangalore	Ward
Richmond	Jamaica	St Mary Parish	
Richmond	Nelsen		
Richmond	Christchurch		Neighborhood
Richmond	KwaZulu-Natal		
Richmond	Northern Cape		
Richmond Hill	Sri Lanka	City of Galle	Neighborhood
Richmond	North Yorkshire	Original Richmond	
Richmond	South Yorkshire	City of Sheffield	
Richmond	Ireland	North Tipperary	Townland
Richmond Harbour	Ireland	Town of Clondra	Neighborhood
Richmond Hill	West Yorkshire	District of Leeds	Neighborhood
Richmond upon Thames	Surrey	Borough of London	
New Richmond	Indiana		
New Richmond	Ohio		
New Richmond	Wisconsin		
Port Richmond	Pennsylvania	Philadelphia	Neighborhood
Richmond	Alabama	Dallas County	
Richmond	California	Contra Costa County	
Richmond	Illinois	McHenry County	
Richmond	Indiana	Wayne County	
Richmond	Iowa	Washington County	Unincorporated
Richmond	Kansas	Franklin County	

Richmond	Kentucky	Madison County	
Richmond	Louisiana		
Richmond	Maine	Sagadahoc County	
Richmond	Massachusetts	Berkshire County	
Richmond	Michigan	Macomb County	
Richmond	Minnesota	Stearns County	
Richmond	Missouri	Ray County	
Richmond	New Hampshire	Cheshire County	
Richmond	New York	Ontario County	
Richmond	Ohio	Jefferson County	
Richmond	Oregon	Portland	Neighborhood
Richmond	Rhode Island	Washington County	
Richmond	South Dakota	Brown County	
Richmond	Tennessee	Bedford County	
Richmond	Texas	Fort Bend County	
Richmond	Utah	Cache County	
Richmond	Vermont	Chittenden County	
Richmond	Virginia	City of Richmond	
Richmond	Wisconsin	St. Croix County	
Richmond	Wisconsin	Shawano County	
Richmond	Wisconsin	Walworth County	
Richmond Beach	Washington	Shoreline	Neighborhood
Richmond County	Georgia		
Richmond County	New York	Staten Island, NYC	Borough
Richmond County	North Carolina		
Richmond County	Virginia		
Richmond Dale	Ohio	Ross County	
Richmond District	California	San Francisco	Neighborhood
Richmond Furnace	Pennsylvania	Franklin County	Metal Township
Richmond Heights	Florida	Miami-Dade County	
Richmond Heights	Missouri		
Richmond Heights	Ohio		
Richmond Hill	Georgia		
Richmond Hill	New York	Queens, NYC	Neighborhood
Richmond Township	Michigan	Macomb County	
Richmond Township	Michigan	Marquette County	
Richmond Township	Michigan	Osceola County	
Richmond Township	Minnesota		
Richmond Township	Ohio	Ashtabula County	
Richmond Township	Ohio	Huron County	
Richmond Township	Pennsylvania	Berks County	
Richmond Township	Pennsylvania	Crawford County	
Richmond Township	Pennsylvania	Tioga County	
Richmondville	New York		Town & Village
University of Richmond	Richmond Virginia		
Richmond, the American International University in London			
Richmond College	Galle, Sri Lanka		

Division of Richmond	Australia	New South Wales	Voting District
Anglican Parish of Richmond	New Brunswick		
Richmond	Arizona	Cochise County	Ghost Town
Richmond	Iowa	Maddison County	Ghost Town
Richmond	Kansas	Franklin County	Ghost Town
Richmond	Kansas	Nemaha County	Ghost Town
Richmond	Missouri	Howard County	Ghost Town
Richmond	Oregon	Wheeler County	Ghost Town
Richmond Hill	Bahamas	Exuma Island	Uninhabited
Richmond River	Australia, New South Wales		
Richmond River	St. Vincent, the Grenadines		
Richmond Lake	Brown County, South Dakota		

RICHMOND FOOTBALL CLUB: FOUNDED 1861

Athletic Ground, Richmond, London, England (Capacity: 2,000). Chairman: Peter Moore
A rugby union club, founding member of the Rugby Football Union and one of the oldest football (of any code) clubs. It fields teams in both men's and women's rugby, with the men's first team playing in National League 1, and the women's first team playing in the women' premiership.

History

Formed in 1861, it is one of the oldest football clubs in the world. It holds a significant place in the history of Association Football, playing in the first ever match on December 19, 1863, against the Barnes Club, even though it was not a member of the Football Association. In 1878 it hosted the first ever floodlit match and in 1909 played in the inaugural match at Twickenham Stadium, the home of English Rugby.

Richmond always traditionally played without a number 13 (similar to Bath) - the Outside Centre would wear 14, Right Wing 15 and Fullback 16. However, during the professional era they adopted Squad Numbering; meaning rather than rugby's usual method of giving numbers 1-15 to the starting lineup, players were assigned a number for the season, as seen in football. Back in the amateur leagues, Richmond returned to their traditional numbering system before promotion to the National Leagues in 2008 saw them forced to adopt the uniform 1-15 numbering system according to RFU laws.

Professional Era

In 1996, the then third division club was bought by financial markets trader and Monaco tax exile Ashley Levett. Levett turned the club into the first professional team in England, and began buying in big names to push the club up the leagues, including Ben Clarke from Bath Rugby, the first £1million signing. The club outgrew the Richmond Athletic Ground and became tenants at the Madejski Stadium in Reading. But the crowds and revenues from competition meant that Levett was continually financing the club, and so he placed it in to administration in March 1999.

The professional Richmond club and professional London Scottish F.C. were both merged into London Irish, who continued to play at the Madejski. This period of hesitancy and uncertainty resulted in many of the professional players leaving the club pre-merger, and returning to their original home-teams. The amateur club was reformed in 2000, and the club rejoined the leagues as an amateur club at the bottom of the pyramid.

Post-Administration

After the professional era, hooker Andy Cuthbert remained at the club and captained the side for several years. Despite its lowly league position, Richmond has still managed to attract some top class players - former South Africa captain Bobby Skinstad joined for the 2005-6 season, Chilean fly-half Sebastian Berti joined in 2006 and England Students' wing Joe Ajuwa was a regular starter in the 1st XV. The club climbed through the lower ranks of the England rugby divisions, from Hertfordshire & Middlesex 1 (ninth level) to London 1 (fifth level) in four years, amassing a perfect record of 83 straight wins in league play in the process. However, the club seemingly stalled at that level, continuing to put together winning seasons, but failing to gain promotion in 2005-6 and 2006-7.

In the 2007-8 season, Richmond laid out a serious plan for promotion - something they had failed to achieve in the past two seasons, one reason being they had not had any semi-professional players on their books. For the 2007-08 season, the club recruited a number of semi-professional players to boost Richmond's promotion chances. One of these players was USA international Jon Hartman. Richmond eventually achieved promotion, winning all but one of their League games, suffering a 1 point defeat away to the runners up, Worthing, in the penultimate game of the season, after promotion had already been guaranteed.

The coach, Brett Taylor, laid out plans for the club to be in National League 2 South in 2 seasons, and attempts were made to structure the colts' teams into an effective feeder system for the 1st XV. However, during summer 2008, London Scottish were boosted financially and subsequently signed Taylor as their head coach. Richmond appointed Geoff Richards to take his place. Following two years in National League Two, Geoff Richards decided not to renew his contract citing differences in opinion between the board and himself on how the club should move forward. In 2009/10 Richmond appointed Oxford University Director of Rugby Steve Hill to take over after 14 years in charge of the university side. Within 2 years promotion was achieved and Richmond will play in National League 1 in 2012/13.

Richmond's youth section is also highly successful - London Irish fullback Delon Armitage was a member of the mini section, and London Wasps' centre Dominic Waldouck earned an England call-up for the 2008 tour of New Zealand, having progressed through the age groups at Richmond. London Wasps No.8 Hugo Ellis, another product of Richmond's youth section, captained Wales U16s, as well as England at U19 and was the England U20 Captain in the 2008 Grand Slam winning side, also reaching the finals of the IRB Junior World Championship. Yet another former Richmond Youth, Joe Simpson, winning his first full England cap in 2011 Rugby World Cup, also of London Wasps, was scrum half for the U20s. Simpson was in the England Sevens squad for the first round of the 2007-8 World Series, Sevens being an important stepping stone for the development of the best youth talent.

In the 2009-2010 season a colts' team was revived based on the highly rated U17 age group team of the previous season, and several U19 players returning to further bolster the squad.

They entered the National Colts Cup and having defeated eight opponents most notably Blackheath, they beat former champions Old Northamptonians, 25-12 at Franklin's Gardens.

Richmond play at the Athletic Ground, Richmond, which borders Royal Mid Surrey Golf Club, and is close by to other sporting facilities such as Richmond Swimming Pool, Old Deer Park and also a gym. The complex includes two pitches (pitches 3 & 4) by the front gate, the 1st team pitch and perpendicular to that, pitch 2. The site also has a disused driving range behind the 1st team pitch which has three pitches on it, and a disused bowls club. One side of the pitch has a large concrete all-seater stand, under which are the changing rooms, a canteen, shop, physio room and two bars. Also on this Southern side of the pitch is a disused cricket pavilion which also contains several more changing rooms and showers. During the early professional years, a temporary stand was erected along the north side of the pitch.

Later on in the professional era, Richmond 1st team moved to the Madejski Stadium, Reading, where they played until bankruptcy. The stadium would later become London Irish's home ground, and was an early example of London rugby clubs playing in football grounds - London Wasps played at Loftus Road before moving to Adams Park, and Saracens moved to Vicarage Road.

Richmond contested the first ever rugby match with Blackheath F.C., and though the clubs are not in the same league, they play an annual pre-season friendly to uphold the tradition.

Richmond share the Athletic Ground with London Scottish, and this rivalry is very intense. Both sides experienced a high point at the beginning of the professional era and played in the Premiership. Both teams also fell into administration and dropped down to a level well below the national leagues, and though the routes taken have been slightly different, both clubs have battled their way up the leagues, until the upcoming season played in the same division - National 3 South. In years when the clubs are in the same division, the two "home" and "away" matches are two of the most well-attended and hotly contested of the year.

Richmond also has a local rivalry with Barnes who they have recently frequently played as both sides sought to move into the national leagues.

At youth level, Richmond's strongest rivalry tends to be with nearby Rosslyn Park. A Richmond vs Rosslyn Park game is always surrounded by controversy of some sort.

(Source: Wikipedia)

Richmond v Blackheath: the oldest two rugby union teams in the world; Richmond won April 13 2013.

Richmond, London President Nick Preston meeting Ian Robertson, Richmondshire Rugby Club from Richmond, Yorkshire at Tynedale Rugby club. Richmondshire are having a new clubhouse built ready Sept/Oct 2013.

Richmond, London have kindly offered to send a team up to open the New Clubhouse. These teams have never played each other in 150 years.

HMS *RICHMOND* (F239)

HMS *Richmond* is a Type 23 Frigate of the Royal Navy. She was launched on 6 April 1993 by Lady Hill-Norton, wife of the late Admiral of the Fleet, The Lord hill Norton, and was the last warship to be built by Swan Hunters Ship Builders. She sailed from the builders on the River Tyne in November 1994.

Deployments

Richmond was first deployed in 1997 to the Far East as part of the 'Ocean Wave 97' Task Group. One of the most interesting visits she made was to the Russian port of Vladivostok, an important Russian naval base, where she became the first Royal Navy vessel to visit in over 100 years. Also that year, *Richmond* escorted the royal yacht Britannia on the ship's final leg of her final tour of the UK prior to her decommissioning.

In 1998 *Richmond* participated in two significant NATO naval exercises and arrived in New York where she was involved in the US Navy Fleet Week. In 1999 *Richmond* was dispatched to the South Atlantic as part of Atlantic Patrol Task South and underwent a major overhaul which concluded in 2000. In 2001 *Richmond* joined the NATO multi-national squadron Standing Naval Force Mediterranean. In 2002 she arrived in the Caribbean where she performed tasks including obligatory "fly-the-flag" duties to the Commonwealth countries in the region as well as undergoing trials.

In 2003, under the command of Commander Wayne Keble, she deployed to the Persian Gulf on Armilla Patrol where she relieved HMS Cardiff. She had arrived shortly before the 2003 Iraq war. When hostilities began, *Richmond*, HM ships Chatham Marlborough and HMAS Anzac of the Royal Australian Navy provided Naval Gunfire Support (NGS) during the Royal Marines amphibious assault of the Al Faw peninsula, the first amphibious assault by the Marines since the Falklands War in 1982. *Richmond* remained in the region at the war's end and returned home in August.

In July 2004, under the command of Commander Mike Mc Cartain, *Richmond* deployed on Atlantic Patrol Task north, which encompasses the Atlantic and Caribbean regions. Two of the ports she visited early in the deployment were Jamaica and Belize. In September *Richmond* came to the assistance of the Turks and Caicos Islands when they were struck by Hurricane Frances. Fortunately the Turks and Caicos Islands suffered only minimal damage to buildings. *Richmond* then sailed to Curacao, Netherlands Antilles where she resumed her maintenance period, which had been interrupted due to the hurricane, but remained on standby to provide assistance due to the imminent arrival of Hurricane Ivan.

Hurricane Ivan eventually hit the region, causing significant damage and fatalities, particularly inflicting enormous damage and unfortunately a number of fatalities to Grenada, which included immense damage to the capital St Georges. *Richmond* and her accompanying Royal Fleet Auxiliary vessel Wave Ruler came to the assistance of the island. The extent of the damage in Grenada reached such levels that Keith Mitchell, Prime Minister of Grenada, was forced to relocate to *Richmond* after his residence was destroyed by the hurricane. The Prime Minister effectively ran his country from *Richmond* for several hours.

Her crew having performed vital assistance on land at Grenada, *Richmond* steamed at her top speed for Jamaica to assist that country in recovering from the ravages of Hurricane Ivan.

Richmond returned from her deployment in December 2004, and began a refit period at HM Naval Base Portsmouth in mid-2005. The refit, undertaken by Fleet Support Limited, was completed in late 2006 and *Richmond* was returned to the operational fleet in October 2006. With 44 major upgrades to her sensor and weapon systems, *Richmond* was at that time one of the most capable Type 23 frigates. From 5 to 12 July 2010 she anchored beside HMS Belfast London to foster the ship's relations with the Borough of Richmond upon Thames

In 2011, she is deployed to the Middle East and the Asia-Pacific region, the latter for upcoming Five Power Defence Arrangement Exercises, specifically Exercise Bersama Shiled 11. She assisted with anti-piracy operations with the EU Naval Force and was also a participant in the IMEX Asia 2011 After Singapore, she rendered honours to the fallen of Force Z .She is due to take part in exercise FRUKUS 2011 with ships from the US Navy and Russian navy

Affiliations

- His grace the Duke of Richmond and Gordon
- The Yorkshire Regiment 14th 15th 19th 33rd/ 76 Foot
- Worship Company of Basket-makers
- Town of Richmond
- Richmond Upon Thames

GUIDE TO RICHMOND YORKSHIRE - A BRIEF HISTORY

Pre-Historic settlers and later discoveries

Neolithic Period (-2000-4000 B.C.) Flints (shaped stones for hunting and shaping tools) Excavated at Scorton near Richmond.

Bronze Age (-2500 - 2000 B.C.)

1992 Bronze Sword found near Catterick Bridge.

Iron Age (-700 B.C. - 1st Century A.D.)

Remains of major earthwork at Malden Castle near Healaugh, Swaledale.

1951-1952 Stanwick earthworks near Aldborough St. John, near Richmond, excavated by Sir Mortimer Wheeler. These fortifications were constructed by the Brigantes, the largest tribe in the North of England in the Iron Age. Their Queen was Cartismadua, who is thought to have made a treaty with the Romans. Roman pottery and artifacts were excavated.

Roman Period (-43 A.D - 400 A.D)

1724 Major Roman hoard found in Richmond Castle bank, 620 silver Roman coins and spoons.
1937 Robert Pedley of Grinton, Swaledale found Roman pottery.

- Amongst this was Samian Ware, a reddish-coloured, high-quality pottery of Roman/Gaul origin.
- Caractonium - A Roman site, possibly present Catterick. Wood writing slabs found at Hadrian's Wall show details of supply requirements sent to Caractonium.
- Fremlington, Swaledale, finds of Roman metal work - now in the British Museum.
- Roman lead mining at Hurst, Swaledale, recorded.
  1956 More Roman coins found in Richmond Castle bank area.

Other Local Finds

1930s Easby Cross (Christian) found at Easby near Richmond. A cast of the original cross is in Easby church. (The original is in the Victoria and Albert Museum.)

1976 Gilling West, Richmond, Viking sword with a silver hilt found in local beck. It is now in Castle Museum, York,

Anglo-Saxon cross found in Gilling Beck and 10th Century Hog-Back Tombstone found at Gilling -West. (Both are now in Richmondshire Museum.)

Roman road of Dere Street which is part of present A1 runs north via Catterick.

Watling Street, a major Roman road, runs north via Stanwick, Durham and Northumberland to Hadrian's Wall.

Invasions to Richmond /Swaledale (-500 A.D. -1000 A.D.)

The Romans gradual withdrawal to other parts of their Empire left England in a state of instability. In Richmond / Swaledale, Anglo-Saxon invaders came first, then later the Danes and Norseman landed. The river Swale and hinterland became part of the kingdom of Deira. Later this was joined to The Kingdom of Bernicia and formed the large kingdom of Northumbria.

570 A.D. Anglo-Saxon battle against local inhabitants at Cattraeth (generally accepted as present Catterick) which defeated the locals.

Christianity later came to the area when monk Paulinus baptised Edwin, King of Northumbria. Hundreds of people were later baptised in the River Swale at a point near Catterick. (Known as The Holy River and the Jordan of England).

Origins of place names

DANISH:

Skeeby, Easby, near Richmond (-BY ending means village)

NORSE:

Upper Swaledale Villages; Thwaite, Muker, Smarber, Satron, Gunnerside, Melbecks, Skaleflat. Lower Swaledale; Marrick, Owlands, Applegarth.

Danish settlements in late 800 A.D. turned to arable farming in lowlands. Norse settlements kept to uplands farming, grazing sheep and cattle.

Norman Era 1066

Richmond, North Yorkshire is the Mother of all Richmonds throughout the world. There are **55** altogether. The word Richmond comes from the Norman Riche-Mont meaning Strong Hill.

1066 William I gave extensive lands to his followers, as a reward for their active support. Alan Rufus of Brittany, a kinsman of William, received the honour of Richmond, which spread over Yorkshire and throughout England, even to parts of Dorset.

1071 Alan Rufus began building the castle. It was built of stone from the outset. A defensive site was chosen on a steep hill above the fast flowing River Swale.

Mid 12th Century Conan 'The Little' Earl of Richmond and Duke of Brittany, added The Great Keep, which was finished by Henry II. It has never been besieged, but in 1174 it was used to imprison the Scottish King, William the Lion.

Medieval Richmond - late 13th, 14th & 15th Centuries

Important growth in wealth led to Richmond becoming a chartered borough. It had 13 craft guilds (which controlled trade.) It had important markets and fairs. Two craft guilds exist to this present day. A market is still held every Saturday. (1441 Henry IV granted a royal charter to hold a Saturday market.)

1311 Defensive stone walls built to protect the town from Scottish raids. Two postern gates in the town wall still survive; The Bar postern at the top of Cornforth Hill and the other Postern gate remains in Friars Wynd.

The Marketplace A large area, it was originally the outer bailey of the Castle. At this time there stood The Stocks and Pillory, for punishing wrongdoers. Also the Market Cross was a feature in the market. It was a place to gather and a position for selling butter and cheese.

The Market Cross was replaced by the present Obelisk - see Georgian History, below.

The Bubonic Plagues -14th and 15th Centuries Richmond and Swaledale had a series of very wet weather during these years, resulting in poor harvests. Cattle and sheep developed disease which led to the population in 1349 being devastated with Bubonic Plague. Lesser epidemics occurred for the next 100 years. A cemetery at Easby Church has a plague stone. This deadly disease wiped out many of the inhabitants and affected the trade and farming industry.

Medieval Religious Houses Richmond had three chapels in the Castle, Trinity Chapel in the Marketplace, later, St. Mary, The Virgin Parish Church; three Chapels on the outskirts of the town; a College for Chantry Priest; two small Hospitals and an Anchorite's cell, (Maison Dieu Area).

An important religious was the House of the Greyfriars (now only the Bell Tower remains) and the premonstratensian - order of The White Canons at Easby Abbey. A small chapel dedicated to St. James of Compestella existed in what is now St. James Chapel Wynd, which leads from the Green to Bargate.

1536/7 Henry VIII broke allegiance from Rome, which eventually resulted in England becoming English Catholics with Henry Head of the Church. Following this, Henry caused the dissolution of the Monasteries. The Abbey at Easby and The Friary both had their roofs and alters shattered, as well as the kitchens laid waste. (Hence Easby Abbey ruins and the limited ruins of the Friary remain.)

Other Early Richmonds

1485 Henry VII held the title of Earl of Richmond. He re-named his royal palace at Sheen, Surrey, thus making a second Richmond. This one in Surrey is the second oldest and Richmond, Virginia is the third.

Have a look at our Richmonds of the World section on Richmond Online.

Richmond and the English Civil War

Mid 17th Century England was divided, some supporting the Monarchy (Charles I) and others, rule by Parliament.

Richmond, at this time, became the Headquarters of the Scottish Army, (Parliamentarians.) The local inhabitants suffered greatly under their harsh behaviour.

1660 Richmond rejoiced when Charles II was restored to the throne.

Late 17th Century Richmond gradually prospered and the two main industries which expanded in the outlying Dale were lead mining and knitting. The wool, which came from the Swaledale sheep, was rough but waterproof. The wool was brought into Richmond, the market town of the Dale. It was sold to buyers who passed it onto local knitters. (whole families, men, women and children made caps and stockings. These were exported to areas of need such as Holland and Belgium (known as The Low Countries).

Georgian Richmond

Late 17th and 18th Centuries marked Richmond's heyday as new elegant Georgian housing and buildings replaced many of the older medieval buildings. Frenchgate and Newbiggin have Georgian buildings to the present day.

Culloden Tower: Built in 1746 by John Yorke, M.P. for Richmond, to commemorate the Hanovarian victory over the Jacobite Scots at Culloden Moor.

Richmond Green during medieval times, this was the area used for a Tannery, Corn and Fulling Mills, A Brewery and Nail Makers. During the Georgian period it was the site of the Yorke Mansion and Gardens, which are now the site of the Culloden Tower.

Social Scene

Well-to-do families came to Richmond to attend the horse races, which took place at Richmond Race Course. Assemblies, Card Parties and Military Musters were other attractions. The King's Head Hotel, still present in the Marketplace, was the main accommodation for the wealthy tourists.

The King's Head Hotel was built in 1718 for the Bathhurst family, whose wealth came from lead-mining. The town house later became a Hotel in the mid 18th Century. Another leading Hotel - no longer existing, was The Blue Bell (now shops) situated at the bottom of the Marketplace.

1756 The Town Hall Built as a Georgian Assembly Room.

Frances l'Anson - The Lass of Richmond Hill

1766 Born in Leyburn, Wensleydale. Association with Hill House, Richmond, through her maternal grandparents who had occupied the house from 1750-1768. Frances married songwriter, Leonard McNally who composed the famous song, sometimes believed to be about Richmond Hill in Surrey.

The Lass of Richmond Hill
On Richmond Hill there lives a lass
More bright than May-day morn,
Whose charms all others maids' surpass,
A rose without a thorn.
This lass so neat,
With smiles so sweet,
Has won my right good will.
I'd crowns resign to call thee mine,

Sweet lass of Richmond Hill!
Sweet lass of Richmond Hill,
Sweet lass of Richmond Hill,
I'd crowns resign to call thee mine,
Sweet lass of Richmond Hill!
Ye zephyrs gay that fan the air,
And wanton through the grove,
O whisper to my charming fair,
I die for her I love.
How happy will the shepherd be
Who calls this nymph his own!
O may her choice be fix'd on me!
Mine's fix'd on her alone.
[Go and visit The Lass of Richmond Hill Inn on the top of Richmond Hill, London. BS]

1768 John Wesley the founder of the non-conformist sect, preached in the Marketplace. He preached again in 1774 at the east end of Newbiggin and finally in 1786 he preached in Frenchgate.

Castle Walk The Castle Walk was built around the walls. This provided level walking - or Promenading, for the wealthy visitors. Scenic views from the Castle Walk of the river Swale, Fosse waterfall and Billy Bank woods were greatly admired.

Richmond Racecourse Grandstand. Richmond Racecourse Grandstand was built in 1777, by John Carr, an eminent Yorkshire Architect. However, the corners on the racecourse were too tight in the 20th century for modern race horses so the course closed in 1950s but there is talk about rebuilding this wonderful grandstand.

1787: Opening of the re-built Georgian Theatre Royal. Samuel Butler was both actor and Manager of players. This theatre was another popular asset.

Richmond Grammar School Re-founded by Queen Elizabeth I in 1567 stood in the parish churchyard. Replaced by a much larger building (facing the Richmond Batts.) In 1850 two famous Georgian Headmasters; Anthony Temple 1724- 1795 and James Tate 1771-1843. Temple succeeded in getting 29 of his pupils sent to Oxford and Cambridge. James Tate was even more successful and the school became nationally known school for classical learning. Tate sent up many scholars to Cambridge. (Known as Tate's Invincibles.) 21 become Fellows, 13 of them at Trinity College. Later Whig Prime minister, Lord Grey, patronised Richmond Grammar School.

1844-46: Lewis Carroll (real name Charles Ludwidge Dodgson) author of Alice in Wonderland and Through the Looking Glass, attended Richmond Grammar School when his father was Rector at Croft on Tees church, near Richmond.

1771 Old Market Cross Replaced by the present obelisk. It was originally built over a large reservoir, which supplied the townsfolk with drinking water.

1788-9 The Green Bridge (called because it crosses over the river to the Richmond Green) was built. Dates and names of the Mayors of the time are carved on the centre of the bridge. Opposite on the other side is a milestone showing the distances to Askrigg and Lancaster. (This was the start of the Richmond - Lancaster turnpike road.) John Carr, the renowned Yorkshire Georgian Architect designed the bridge.

19th Century

1817 The Thomas Bradley map shows the result of The Enclosures Act of Parliament which affected Richmond; the medieval three fields, West Field, The Gallowfield and East Field ceased to be public. William Dawson supervised the sale of land. The burgage house owners, dominated by the Dundas family who were M.P.s were for the enclosure system.

Municipal Reform 1832 Parliament reformed system of representation.
Richmond now had a Mayor, 4 Aldermen and 12 Councillors. The vote was given to all rate-payers.

Richmond Gas Works 1830 A sub-committee formed to organise first street lighting; 12-18 oil lamps positioned in various parts of the town.

1820 Gas-Light Company was founded, site chosen was near the Fosse (waterfall) and the Castle mill site.

1849 The private gas company was taken over by the Richmond Corporation. Richmond is credited as being a leader of radical reform and one of the first towns to have public street lighting. The Coming of the Railways 1846

The Darlington to Stockton Railway was opened in 1825

A branch line was later extended in 1846 to Richmond chiefly looking for profits from the carriage of coal, lead and lime. The cost of transporting Swaledale lead to Stockton was cut by one third. The farming community benefitted, as grain and crops exported were also cheaper. Nine miles of track was completed in a few months running through Dalton, Moulton, Catterick Bridge, Richmond.

The bridge over the Swale and Station Road leading up to the Marketplace were built around the same time. The railway and station buildings boosted tourist trade into Richmond and also gave the ordinary townsfolk better facility to travel.

Richmond Water Supply 18th and 19th Century

From medieval wells and springs leading water from Westfields to the Marketplace via a lead lined conduit and spring water led into hollowed-out Elm branches - Richmond progressed in 1749 to all lead pipes. Water supply was increased from Aislebeck Springs further to the west. A reservoir was built on Westfields and 1771 the new obelisk replaced the old Market Cross with a large reservoir built below it (capable of holding 12,000 gallons of water.)

1837 Reservoir made at Colesgarth up Gallowfields to increase water supply needed for growth in population. Lord Dundas leased this area to the corporation for 990 years. It was named Victoria Water Supply after the reigning monarch. The new water supply gave 150 gallons per minute.

Catterick Camp Early 20th Century

Lord Baden Powell, (founder of the Boy- Scout Movement) Head of the Northern Division of the Territorials, while living in Richmond Barracks in the Castle in 1908-1910, planned Catterick Camp, to be situated south of Richmond in the Hipswell area. The Camp's first troops occupied the area in 1915. Commander M.F. Rimmington was the officer in charge.

1915 5000 German prisoners of war were housed at the Camp, where they were employed in constructing the road leading out of Richmond Station - via St. Martins- Hipswell Road - The Camp.

1927 June 29th: Plaque in Reeth Road records the Total Eclipse.

1929 600th Anniversary of Town's charters. Celebrated with roasting an Ox in Richmond market place.

War Memorials: 1914-1918 & 1935-1945

1914-18: Situated in Friary Gardens.

Green Howards' War Memorial is situated at the head of Frenchgate.

Museums:

Green Howards' Museum is situated in Richmond Marketplace.

Richmondshire Museum is situated in Ryders Wynd

Georgian Theatre Royal is situated between Fryers Wynd and Victoria Road.

* Please Note - This is not intended to be the definitive guide to the history of Richmond. We are willing to accept additional information or to be corrected where necessary. If you know something that may be of interest please contact us with details.

[I would like to thank Moonburst and Andy Russell for allowing me to use all Richmond on Line information very freely for Richmonds of the World Book: www.richmondonline.co.uk. Many Thanks. BS]

The Company of Mercers, Grocers and Haberdashers of Richmond (Yorkshire) is the senior of the thirteen companies of merchants and craftsmen which flourished in the 15th and 16th Centuries in this ancient Borough and whose arms are featured in the Mayor's chain of office and exhibited above the seat of the chief magistrate in the old Court in the Town Hall. They comprised:

Mercers, Grocers and Haberdashers ; Drapers Vintners and Surgeons; Taylors; Tanners; Glovers and Skinners united under the name Fellmongers; Butchers; Cordwainers and Curriers; Sadlers, Bridlers, Glaziers, Coopers, Bakers, Osiers and Painters; Carpenters and Joiners; Clothiers, Weavers, Fullers and Dyers; Blacksmiths; Masons, Wallers and Lime-burners; Cappers

During the 17th century at least 14 companies existed. In the researches for his book *'The History of the Company of Mercers, Grocers and Haberdashers of Richmond'*, Ralph Waggett, Freeman and Past Warden of the Company, traced a record of 8 June 1669 in which 'John Cowling and Christopher Breaks as Wardens of the Society of Goldsmiths, Armourers, Lorimers, Cutlers, Spurriers and Plummers within the town of Richmond'.

No one knows when the Company was formed but its minutes survive in continuous succession from 1580 to the present day.

The members met to safeguard their trade and their rights and obligations as freemen, then, as commerce and industry developed and the old restraints were seen to be obsolete they met as friends, dining in some style. In the aftermath of the Great War they began to take on their modern aspect of a fraternity upholding their ancient traditions, but developing a concern for education and charitable giving. They dine still, with their Warden in November and February each year and they rejoice in hospitable dealing one with another.

The Company have formed links with many other Gilds in London, York, Chester and other cities in the British Isles. They have a fine collection of silver, which is displayed when they dine and is on permanent display in the Green Howards' Museum. Their Warden invites all present at Dinner to join with him in the ancient ceremony of the Loving Cup

The Arms of the Company are those of the Mercers, Grocers and Haberdashers united in one shield in a play of three. First, the Mercers with their motto Honor Deo. Second, the Grocers whose motto is God Grant Grace and the third, the Haberdashers with their motto, Serve and Obey. The supporters and crest are those of the Grocers Company.

Present Warden Michael A. Pattison

Deputy Warden Dr Michael Nicholls

Clerk Michael Clayson, 11 Whitefields Gate, Richmond, N. Yorks DL10 7DD   **Tel.** 01748 822631

Welcome to the Fellmongers' Company of Richmond, Yorkshire

The Fellmongers' Company of Richmond in Yorkshire is an ancient craft and trading company which has its origin in the Middle-Ages and was originally made up of Skinners and Glovers.

A fellmonger is a dealer in fells or sheepskins, who separates the wool from the pelts.

The Fellmongers probably began as a religious fraternity whose members, drawn from the same occupation, met for worship having their own shrine and observing their own saint's day.

The Richmond Shilling

The practice of the Mayor's Audit Money was first mentioned in the Charter of Queen Elizabeth

1, which was given to the town in 1576. The Town of Richmond, under previous charters, paid to the Crown a sum of money in respect of the Crown land.

In the 1576 Charter the Queen decreed that the money should be returned to the Mayor of the day to be distributed by him to "poor indigenous tradesmen and decayed house-keepers" just before Christmas.

The Queen's decree has been observed since 1576 and is now given to any man or woman, over the age of 60, who is a resident in the town of Richmond.

In 1986 it was decided that the Mayor would issue a specially-minted coin, based on the size of an old florin, which was named the **Richmond Shilling**.

People who qualify can collect theirs from Mayor of Richmond, Oliver Blease, in the Mayor's Parlour in the Town Hall until noon. Their names are recorded in the ledger of Audit Money.

A major source of income for early Dukes of Richmond was the income they received as duty on coal shipped from the River Tyne and paid for their lifestyle and helped them to build Goodwood and Richmond House, London. Edward 3 was the first monarch to allow a charge on coal production and the price for Elizabeth's assent: a one-shilling duty on every domestic chaldron--36 bushels--of coal and five shillings on every exported chaldron. The Crown several decades later transferred all the coal duties to the Duke of Richmond's family, giving rise to the term "Richmond Shilling." It is unclear whether the Richmond Shilling was ever a genuine tax, or a kickback, or a little of both. Either way, the arrangement made the Crown, and later the government, a silent partner in the monopoly. The arrangement, through various royal and governmental ownerships, remained in place for 231 years.

(Source: Richmond Shilling, Saturday, Dec 10, 2011, richmond.org with permission)

Georgian racecourse ruin.

RICHMOND HOUSE, WHITEHALL, LONDON

The origins of the town house of the Lennox family were with the Stuart Dukes of Richmond and Lennox, collateral relations of Charles II. In 1661 a small house had been built on the river bank, on one of Henry VIII's old bastions, probably for Sir Charles Berkeley. By 1667 the enlarged house belonged to Charles Stuart, 3rd Duke of Richmond and Lennox and fourth cousin of the King. In March that year he married the beautiful Frances Teresa Stuart, lady-in-waiting to Queen Catherine. As they eloped from Court, much to the fury of the King, it is unlikely that the young Duke had time to improve the house for his bride before their marriage, but he subsequently either enlarged or rebuilt his marital home. Together they lived at this, the first Richmond House, from August 1668. In the second half of 1672 they were enlarging it again, but that December the Duke died the last of the Stuart Dukes of Richmond and Lennox.

Frances Teresa, the widowed Duchess of Richmond, was left with a dwelling comprising 28 rooms, including substantial offices at the southern end. The house on the river was at the edge of the Bowling Green, a short distance along the line of the river from the end of Whitehall Palace. It was in this nearby corner of the Palace that the spacious 40-room apartments of Louise de Keroualle were at the time situated. She had just given birth to the King's youngest child, Charles Fitzroy, who in 1675 was given a new surname of Lennox and was made Duke of Richmond and Lennox, in a new creation. The quite separate location of the Richmond House of the Stuart family from the palace can clearly be seen, complete with the jutting out bastion, in a survey plan of Whitehall Palace of 1680.

(With permission from Highbeam)

Richmond House is now the home of the Department of Health and is in the heart of Westminster, within walking distance of the Houses of Parliament and various other Government departments. Hence the easiest way to travel there is by the London Underground.

RICHMOND SAUSAGES

Richmond sausages began in 1889 when Mr. Louis Moore set up a small shop at 63 Linacre Road Birmingham, selling his fine sausages. Proving a real hit, the business boomed and in 1917 the first-ever Richmond sausage factory was opened on the same site as the shop. The founding members were Louis, his son Alfred and his brother George Moore.

The empire had begun. In the first week of production, the Moores and one other member of staff produced an incredible 600lbs of sausages — and what's more, they managed to sell every single one! By 1930, the empire had grown even larger, with 230 people producing the now famed sausages and a fleet of 120 vans delivering them to towns and villages.

With the arrival of the Second World War came tremendous hardship for Britain, but business continued to grow; it appeared there was nothing the troops liked better than a good plate of bangers and mash. So the humble Richmond sausage became the pride of the nation — with soldiers throughout Britain enjoying taste of Richmond sausages during the War years.

To this day, the word Richmond is synonymous with the highest quality bangers — gracing tables up and down the country at teatime. We're as proud of Richmond sausages today as we've ever been — their unmatched quality has stood the test of time and they'll be a family favourite for years to come.

Richmond sausages are now produced by Kerry Foods and the HQ is Birmingham, UK.

HISTORY OF ASKE HALL, RICHMOND, YORKSHIRE AND THE DUNDAS FAMILY

The name Aske (or Ash (tree) or Hasse) derives from Scandinavian mythology and was mentioned as a manor in the Domesday Book. The de Ask family, descended from Whyomar, a kinsman of Earl Alan, lived at Aske until the early 16th Century. The property then passed to the Bowes family who sold it to Lord Wharton who became the Duke of Wharton but went spectacularly bust in 1727 and Aske was sold to Sir Conyers D'Arcy. Sir Conyers lived at Aske for the next 30 years and died in 1758, leaving Aske to his nephew, the last Earl of Holderness.

Sir Lawrence Dundas, Baronet. (1712-1781) bought the Aske Estate from Lord Holderness in 1763 for £45,000 and the imposing Hall has remained the family seat ever since.

Sir Lawrence was a hugely ambitious and successful man and one of the reasons he bought Aske was that the estate included the pocket borough of Richmond and he was therefore able to nominate the MP. He married Margaret Bruce.

Sir Lawrence made his first fortune by supplying goods to the British Army during their campaign against the Jacobites and then in Flanders during the Seven Years War, 1756-1763. He subsequently branched out into banking, property (he developed Grangemouth in 1777) and was a major backer of the Forth and Clyde Canal which happened to run through his Estate at Kerse near Falkirk.

Despite his best endeavours, Sir Lawrence never made it to the peerage but his son Thomas was created Baron Dundas of Aske in 1794. The 1st Lord Dundas (1741-1820) married Lady Charlotte FitzWilliam, who provided him with additional social respectability and a great many children. He was Lord Lieutenant of Orkney and Zetland, MP for Richmond (1763-1768) and MP for Stirling (1768-1794). He was succeeded by his eldest son Lawrence.

In return for providing financial assistance to the Duke and Duchess of Kent, the future Queen Victoria's parents, the 2nd Lord Dundas (1766-1839) was created the 1st Earl of Zetland in 1838. Sir Lawrence Dundas, his grandfather, had bought many estates and among them (again for Parliamentary purposes) was an estate on Orkney and Zetland, which is now better known as Shetland. Thus, when Lawrence was promoted to the Earldom, he chose Zetland as the name for his new title. He was, during his career, Lord Lieutenant and Vice-Admiral of Orkney and Zetland. He married Harriot, daughter of General John Hale.

His son Thomas Dundas (1795-1873) succeeded as 2nd Earl of Zetland. He was a Knight of the Garter, Lord Lieutenant of the North Riding of Yorkshire and Grandmaster of the Freemasons of England. He was also the fortunate owner of Voltigeur, a great racehorse, who won the Derby and St Leger in 1850. The following year, Voltigeur and The Flying Dutchman, owned by the Earl of Eglington and Winton and winner of the 1851 Derby, raced each other at York for 1,000 guineas in what became known as The Great Match. The Flying Dutchman won. The 2nd Earl married Sophia Williamson, daughter of Sir Hedworth Williamson, Baronet but died childless.

His nephew Lawrence Dundas (1844-1929) became the 3rd Earl of Zetland and subsequently, the 1st Marquess of Zetland. He married Lady Lillian Lumley, daughter of the 9th Earl of Scarbrough. He was promoted to the marquesate in 1892 following his term of office as Lord

Lieutenant of Ireland between 1889-1892. In addition, he was a Knight of the Thistle, MP for Richmond, Mayor of Richmond and a Lord-in-Waiting to Queen Victoria.

The 1st Marquess was succeeded by his son, another Lawrence Dundas (1876-1961), as 2nd Marquess of Zetland. This Lawrence had an impressive career in public service first as MP for Hornsey in Middlesex 1907 - 1916, then as Governor of Bengal 1917 - 1922 and finally as Secretary of State for India between 1935 & 1940. He was also president of the Royal Geographical Society, the first chairman of the National Trust, a Governor of the National Bank of Scotland, a Knight of the Garter and Privy Councillor. He bore the Sword of State at the coronation of King George VI in 1937. He married Cicely, daughter of Col. Archdale.

Lawrence Aldred Mervyn Dundas, the 3rd Marquess of Zetland, (1908-1988) succeeded his father in 1961. He was a member of the Jockey Club, Chairman of both Redcar and Catterick Racecourses and a vice president of the All England Lawn Tennis and Croquet Club as he had been a good enough player to have taken part in the Wimbledon championships in the 1940s. He carried out substantial alterations to Aske Hall which resulted in a greatly reduced but much more manageable house. He married Penelope, daughter of Colonel Ebenezer Pike and they have four children: the present Marquess, Lady Serena Kettlewell, Lord David Dundas, the composer and singer and Lord Bruce Dundas.

This work on Aske Hall has been continued by Lawrence Mark Dundas, the 4th (born in 1937) and present Marquess of Zetland. The 4th Marquess has been involved with the administration of British racing for many years, is a member of the Jockey Club and was a founding member of the British Horseracing Board. He married Susan, daughter of Guy Chamberlin and they have four children: Earl of Ronaldshay, Lord James Dundas, Lady Henrietta Stroyan and Lady Victoria Madel.

Aske Hall. Photo courtesy of Jerry Hardman-Jones.

EASBY HALL, RICHMOND, NORTH YORKSHIRE

High on a bank of the River Swale this classic Georgian country house overlooks the ruins of Easby Abbey and the ancient church of St Agatha's. This unrivaled view must have inspired the Reverend William Smith to build the first Easby Hall in 1729 - the 3 floor, 5 bay core of the current house.

The Reverend Smith died in 1735 aged 85 and Leonard Jacques bought the estate for £5,700 to begin the Jacques family's long association with Easby. The Jacques family owned the manor of Easby Hall and the title Lords of the Manor for over 220 years from 1732 until 1955 and made their money from steel in Teesside. The patriarch's grandson, also Leonard, was still in residence in 1911 (he built the South Wing which bears his initials, in 1900) and died in 1916. Leonard's eldest son Robert Harold Wetham Jacques became heir to the estate and in 1933 with his driver Ernest John Johnson he drove Monte Carlo Rally in a Rolls Royce and whilst gambling he is reputed to have broken the Bank. Foundations were dug to build a new Easby Hall but Jacques lost his money gambling so it never got built. In 1955 John Simpson bought the estate from a Major Goldingham who was the husband of Leonard Jacques' daughter Agatha Leonora.

The Simpson family owned Easby Hall from 1955 to 1980 and ran it as a working farm. In 1980, the North Wing, originally the butler's and servants quarters was separated from the house and the old stone steps and entrance to the cellar was covered over and converted into two apartments. The present owners, John and Karen Clarke, have carried out an extensive restoration programme and returned the house to a single dwelling.

The 30-room house has finally regained its original Georgian layout and the North Wing now offers 3 sumptuous suites for bed and breakfast. During the Clarke's restoration the gardens were also returned to their original use to create an authentic kitchen garden from which guests enjoy organic fruit and compotes for breakfast. In addition, there is a scented herbaceous walled garden and the abbey garden with its sweeping infinity lawn and stunning vista of the 12th century abbey, St Agatha's and Richmond castle in the distance; a view that Reverend Smith would recognize today.

BOLTON CASTLE, RICHMONDSHIRE

Enjoy the Ultimate Medieval Experience in the historic heart of Wensleydale part of Richmondshire, Yorkshire. This magnificent medieval fortress is steeped in history and has something for all the family to enjoy including falconry experience, archery, wild boar and much more.

Bolton Castle provides a huge range of exciting things to do in Wensleydale, Yorkshire. From family days out to educational trips and historic tours you will find a raft of sights, sounds and smells which bring the castle to life and make for a truly memorable trip.

Bolton Castle is one of the country's best preserved medieval castles; originally built as one of the finest and most luxurious homes in the land. The castle is still in the private ownership of Lord Bolton, the direct descendant of the castle's original owner Sir Richard le Scrope.

Completed in 1399, its scars bear testament to over 600 years of fascinating history including involvement in the Pilgrimage of Grace, Mary Queen of Scot's imprisonment and a Civil War siege. Bolton Castle was a grand family home as well as a defensive fortress and, despite being partially 'slighted' by Cromwell's' men during the Civil War siege, is still preserved in outstanding condition with many interesting rooms and features to discover including the Old Kitchens, Dungeon, Solar, Nursery, Armory, Great Chamber and Mary Queen of Scots' bedroom. About one third of the rooms are fully intact and the rest of the Castle is almost completely accessible giving visitors great insight into its turbulent past.

We give our visitors a taste of what life was really like during the Castle's heyday through providing the sights, sounds, smells and experiences of life in the past with our wonderful falconry displays, archery demonstrations, wild boar, bees, rare breed sheep and hands on crafts and games.

Visitors often comment on the incredible atmosphere of the Castle with many of the rooms giving the feeling that their inhabitants had just walked out.

Other highlights include:

- Children's costumes, trails, Activity Books and Activity Packs available for younger
- visitors
- Medieval Nursery with games and toys
- Beautiful gardens and maze
- Tea room serving locally sourced and home-made cakes, snacks and light lunches.
- Group tours, packages and special booking rate available (groups over 15 persons)

New for 2013

New Owls and Kites

We will be welcoming several new birds to our flying team including an enormous Turkmenian Owl and tiny Southern White-Faced Scop's owl as well a magnificent Kite who will add a new dimension to our falconry displays.

Interpretation

We are also introducing several new information boards including a Castle time-line, a family tree and two fantastic illustrations of the Castle showing how it would have looked in 1399 and how it looks today.

Opening times 2013:

Open daily 10am – 5pm from 16th February until November 3rd 2013 (Open until 6pm during summer holidays).

Please note: we will close early on the following dates (usually Saturdays) due to weddings. Our last entry will be at 1pm and we will close at 2pm on: 30th March, 13th April, 5th May (3pm close), 1st, 8th June, and 3rd August.

RABY CASTLE, STAINDROP, DURHAM

Set within a 250 acre deer park, with beautiful walled gardens, Raby Castle was built by the mighty Nevilles in the 14th Century, and has been home to Lord Barnard's family since 1626. Open to visitors seasonally between May and September, the Castle rooms display fine furniture, impressive artworks, and elaborate architecture. The Castle hosts a number of popular events each year including an annual Orchid Show, Classic Vehicle Shows, outdoor theatre, markets and children's events.

(Credit: Raby Castle, Co Durham, the home of Lord Barnard, opens to visitors seasonally between May and September. Copyright Raby Castle/Heritage House Media Ltd).

'I had ambition , not only to go further than anyone had been before, but as far as it was possible for man to.' Captain James Cook, RN, born Whitby, North Yorkshire

HISTORY OF THE DUKEDOM

Duke of Richmond, named after Richmond and its surrounding district of Richmondshire, is a title in the Peerage of England that has been created four times in British history. It has been held by members of the Royal Tudor and Stuart families.

1ˢᵗ Duke

The first creation of a Dukedom of Richmond (as Duke of Richmond and Somerset) was made in 1525 for Henry Fitzroy, an illegitimate son of King Henry VIII. His mother was Elizabeth Blount. Upon the Duke's death without children in 1536, his titles it became extinct.

2ⁿᵈ Duke

The second creation was in 1623 for Ludovic Stuart, 2nd Duke of Lennox (1574–1624), who also held other titles. He was created Earl of Richmond in 1613 and Duke of Richmond in the peerage of England in 1623 as a member of the Lennox line (not unlike King James himself) in the house of Stuart. These became extinct at his death in 1624, but his Scottish honours devolved on his brother Esme Earl of March who thus became 3rd Duke of Lennox in the peerage of Scotland.

3ʳᵈ Duke

Esmé's son James 4ᵗʰ Duke of Lennox (1612–1655) subsequently received the third creation of the Dukedom of Richmond in 1641, when the two Dukedoms again became united. In 1672, on the death of James' nephew Charles, 3rd Duke of Richmond and 6th Duke of Lennox, both titles again became extinct.

4ᵗʰ Duke

The fourth creation of the Dukedom of Richmond was in August 1675, when Charles II granted the title to Charles Lennox his illegitimate son by Louise de Keroualle, Duchess of Portsmouth. Charles Lennox was further created Duke of Lennox a month later. Charles' son, also Charles, succeeded to the French title Duke of Aubigny of Aubigny sur Nere on the death of his grand-mother in 1734. The 6th Duke of Richmond and Lennox was created Duke of Gordon in 1876. Thus, the Duke holds three (four, if the French Aubigny claim is accepted) Dukedoms, more than any other person in the realm.

The subsidiary titles of the Dukedom created in 1675 are: Earl of March (created 1675), Earl of Darnley (1675), Earl of Kinrara (1876), Baron Settrington of Settrington in the County of York (1675) and Lord Torbolton (1675).

The Dukes of Richmond, Lennox and Gordon are normally styled Duke of Richmond and Gordon. Before the creation of the Dukedom of Gordon they were styled Duke of Richmond and Lennox. The titles Earl of March and Baron Settrington were created in the peerage of England along with the Dukedom of Richmond. The titles Earl of Darnley and Lord Torbolton were created in the Peerage of Scotland along with the Dukedom of Lennox. Finally, the title Earl of Kinrara was created in the peerage of the United Kingdom with the Dukedom of Gordon. The eldest son of the Duke uses the Courtesy title Earl of March and Kinrara. Before the creation of the Dukedom of Gordon, the courtesy title used was Earl of March.

The family seat is Goodwood House near Chichester West Sussex.

The heir apparent is Charles Gordon Lennox Earl of March (b. 1955), only son of the 10th Duke. The heir apparent to the heir apparent is Charles Gordon-Lennox, Lord Settrington (b. 1994), eldest son of Lord March.

Charles Lennox, 1st Duke of Richmond

Charles Lennox, 1st Duke of Richmond, 1st Duke of Lennox, 1st Duke of Aubigny

(29 July 1672 – 27 May 1723) Illegitimate son of Charles II of England and his mistress Louise de Kerouaille, Duchess of Portsmouth.

Lennox was created Duke of Richmond Earl March and Baron Settringham in the Peerage of England on 9 August 1675 and Duke of Lennox Earl Darley and Lord Torbolton in the Peerage of Scotland on 9 September 1675, and was invested as a Knight of the Garter in 1681. He was appointed Lord High Admiral under reservation of the commission granted to James Duke of Albany and York (later James VII), as Lord High Admiral for life. The appointment was therefore only effective between 1701 and 1705, when Lennox resigned all his Scottish lands and offices.

It appears that he was Master of a Lodge in Chichester in 1696, and so was one of the few known seventeenth century Freemasons.

Family

He was married to Anne Brudenell (died 9 December 1722) daughter of Francis, Baron Brudenell on 8 January 1692 with whom he had three children. He is an ancestor of Diana Princess of Wales, Camilla Duchess of Cornwall and Sarah Ferguson Duchess of York.

Early life

Lennox was styled Earl of March from his birth in 1701 as heir to his father's Dukedom. He also inherited his father's love of sports, particularly cricket. He had a serious accident aged 12 when he was thrown from a horse during a hunt, but he recovered and it did not deter him from horsemanship.

March was entered into an arranged marriage in December 1719 when he was still only 18 and his bride, Lady Sarah Cadogan was just 13. They were married at The Hague.

In 1722, March became Member of Parliament for Chichester as first member with Sir Thomas Miller as his second. He gave up the post after his father died in May 1723 and he succeeded to the title of 2nd Duke of Richmond. A feature of Richmond's career was the support he received from his wife Sarah, her interest being evident in surviving letters. Their marriage was a great success, especially by Georgian standards. Their grandson who became the 4th Duke is known to cricket history as the Honourable Colonel Charles Lennox, a noted amateur batsman of the late 18th century who was one of Thomas Lord's main guarantors when he established his new ground in Marylebone.

Richmond was born at Gordon Castle, near Fochabers, Scotland, the son of General Lord George Lennox, the younger son of Charles Lennox 2nd Duke of Richmond. His mother was Lady Louisa, daughter of William Kerr 4th Marquess of Lothian.

Cricket

Richmond was a keen cricketer. He was an accomplished right-hand bat and a noted wicketkeeper. An amateur, he was a founder member of the Marylebone cricket club. In 1786, together with the earl of Winchelsea, Richmond offered Thomas lord a guarantee against any losses Lord might suffer on starting a new cricket ground. This led to Lord opening his first cricket ground in 1787. Although Lords Cricket Ground has since moved twice, Lennox' and Winchelsea guarantee provided the genesis of the best-known cricket ground in the world, a ground known as the Home of Cricket. Nearly always listed as the Hon. Colonel Charles Lennox in contemporary scorecards, Lennox had 55 recorded first-class appearances from 1784 to 1800 and played a few more games after that.

Army General

Richmond became a British Army captain at the age of 23 in 1787. On 17 May 1789, while a colonel in the Duke of York's regiment, he was involved in a duel with Frederick Duke of York, who had expressed the opinion that "Colonel Lennox had heard words spoken to him at Daughbigny's, to which no gentleman ought to have submitted", effectively an accusation of failing to respond to an insult in the way that a gentleman should. At Wimbledon Common, Lennox fired, but his ball "grazed his Royal Highness's curl"; the Duke did not fire.

Colonel Lennox shortly after exchanged his company for the commission of Lieutenant-Colonel in the 35th Regiment of Foot. On 1 July of the same year, he was involved in another duel, with Theophilus Swift, Esquire in consequence of a pamphlet criticising Lennox's character published under Swift's name. They met in a field near the Uxbridge Road, where Swift was wounded in the body, but recovered.

Lennox was also MP for Sussex, succeeding his father, from 1790 until he succeeded to the Dukedom.

Duke

He became the 4th Duke of Richmond on 29 December 1806, after the death of his uncle, Charles Lennox 3rd Duke of Richmond. In April 1807 he became Lord of Lieutenant of Ireland. He remained in that post until 1813, with Arthur Wellesley (the later Duke of Wellington) as his secretary. He participated in the Napoleonic Wars and in 1815 he was in command of a reserve force in Brussels, which was protecting that city in case Napoleon won the Battle of Waterloo. On 15 June, the night before the Battle of Quatre Bras, his wife held a Ball for his fellow officers. Although he observed the battle the next day, as well as Waterloo on 18 June, he did not go to the Ball.

Governor General of Canada

In 1818 he was appointed Governor General of British North America.

During the summer of 1819, Richmond undertook an extensive tour of Upper and Lower Canada. At William Henry (Sorel, Quebec) he was bitten on the hand by a pet fox. The injury apparently healed, and he continued to York (Toronto) and Niagara (Niagara-on-the-Lake, Ontario), even examining military sites as far distant as Drummond Island. Returning to Kingston, he planned a leisurely visit to the settlements on the Rideau. During this part of the journey the first symptoms of hydrophobia appeared. The disease developed rapidly and on 28 August he died in extreme agony in a barn a few miles from a settlement that had been named in his honour. Some accounts suggest that the Duke had been bitten by a dog; stronger contemporary evidence, however, supports the view that he had received the rabies infection from a fox.

The night before his death, he slept at the "Masonic Arms" a tavern in Richmond, Ontario owned by Andrew Hill (former Sergeant. Major of the 100th Regiment of Foot) and Maria Hill, his wife and heroine of the War of 1812. After the Duke of Richmond's death, Maria prepared his body to be sent back to Quebec City for burial and Hill's tavern was renamed the "Duke of Richmond Arms" to commemorate the visit. Lennox's title was inherited by his son, Charles Gordon Lennox, 5th Duke of Richmond. Lennox was given a state funeral in Quebec City on 4th September, and he is buried in the city's Anglican Holy Trinity Cathedral.

Legacy

Richmond's legacy was not inconsiderable and besides other places, he had following places named after him:

- Richmond, Quebec
- Richmond County, Nova Scotia
- Richmond Street in Toronto, Ontario
- According to tradition, the town of Richmond Hill, Ontario, was also named after him, as he was said to have passed through the then village during his visit in 1819.

Name (b/d)	Dates as Duke	Married	
5th Duke	Charles Gordon-Lennox 1791-1860	1819-1860	Lady Caroline Paget
6th Duke	Charles Henry Gordon-Lennox 1818-1903	1860-1903	Lady Francis Greville
7th Duke	Charles Henry Gordon-Lennox 1845-1928	1903-1928	Widowed
8th Duke	Charles Henry Gordon-Lennox 1870-1935	1928-1935	Hilda Brassey
9th Duke	Frederick Charles Gordon-Lennox		
1904-1935	1935-1989	Elizabeth Hudson	
10th Duke	Charles Henry Gordon-Lennox b 1929	1989 -	Susan Greville-Grey

Goodwood House, Sussex.

GOODWOOD HOUSE

Goodwood House is a country house in west Sussex in Southern England. It is the seat of the Dukes of Richmond. Several architects have contributed to the design of the house, including James Wyatt. It was the intention to build the house to a unique octagonal layout, but only three of the eight sides were built. Some of the older parts of the house also survive, although some sections were demolished in the mid-20th century. The house has opulent neo-classical interiors and is open to the public on a limited number of days per year. It is also available to hire for weddings and corporate events.

Goodwood, one of the finest stately homes in the country, has been the home of the Dukes of Richmond and Lennox for over 300 years. The 1st Duke of Richmond was the natural son of King Charles II and his French mistress, Louise de Keroualle. He originally bought Goodwood as a hunting lodge and subsequent Dukes enlarged the existing Jacobean house to create the magnificent house that we see today, set in mature parkland against the backdrop of the Sussex Downs. The architects Roger Morris, Matthew Brettingham and James Wyatt were all involved at various stages during the eighteenth and early nineteenth centuries. Goodwood, like many other stately homes, has an outstanding art collection, formed by successive generations of the family, which includes paintings by Van Dyck, Canaletto, Stubbs and Reynolds, Sèvres porcelain, Gobelins' tapestries and eighteenth-century French and English furniture.

The surrounding Goodwood Estate is a major sport and leisure venue featuring Goodwood Racecourse, home of the Glorious Goodwood flat-racing festival, which is one of the highlights of the English social season; Chichester Goodwood Airport and Goodwood Classic; and the Goodwood Park Hotel, Golf and Country Club. The immediate grounds of the house also play host to the annual Goodwood Festival of Speed, which has rapidly become a major event in the diary of all fans, participants and companies associated with motor racing. The Rolls Royce motor cars manufacturing plant is located on the south end of Goodwood Estate.

Within the grounds is a golf course, as well as a members' only clubhouse known as The Kennels, originally built for the hounds of the 3rd Duke of Richmond. Outside the grounds is the hotel, formerly a franchise of Marriott and now independently run by the Goodwood Company.

In 1982, the Goodwood estate played host to the World Road Cycling Championship. The women's race was won by Great Britain's Mandy Jones, while the men's professional race was won by Guiseppe Saronni, who launched a devastating sprint in the final 300 metres to overtake the USA's Greg Lemond (who would win the title the following year) and local favourite, Sean Kelly from Ireland.

The Monarchs' Way (long-distance footpath) crosses the Downs from west to east, passing immediately south of the racecourse. The Goodwood House also looks directly over the cricket pitch, home to the Goodwood Cricket Club. (Source: for Duke of Richmond: Wikipedia)

TWINNING TOWNS

Richmond is twinned with two towns, one in France, the other in Norway. Our French twin is Saint Aubin du Cormier in Brittany. It's a market town perched on a hill, rather like Richmond, but the strongest links are between the two castles which once defended each community.

Richmond Castle was built in 1071 by a French noble who had been given the land by William the Conqueror. Now move forward 150 years and meet the 8th Earl of Richmond, Pierre de Dreux. He admired his Yorkshire castle so much that he went over to Brittany and built another like it and this was the beginning of Saint Aubin du Cormier.

What Does Twinning Mean for the People of Richmond?

Making links with our French twin town results in a lot of fun and new friendships. Pupils from Richmond School have exchanged visits with their counterparts at Pierre de Dreux College. Primary schools are beginning to make links.

Richmond Mavericks Football Club has been over to play matches against the St. Aubin team and the French players visited our town in the summer of 2008.

The French Twinning Agreement was signed only in 2006 and the Association wants to help other Richmond organisations to make links with their equivalent in Saint Aubin.

Associations make exchange visits every other year and the St Aubin visitors came here in April 2009. This is all done on a very low budget, with families opening their homes to guests and members paying most of their own travel expenses. Our French friends have always given us a very warm welcome. The last visit by members of the Richmond Association was in 2011.

Saint Aubin Du Cormier France, Today

Saint Aubin is about 17 miles from Rennes, the regional capital, and is an attractive market town perched on a rocky crest in the Breton Marches. About 3,500 people live there. It's a mainly agricultural economy and the French Marines have a base nearby, so it has some of the garrison town qualities of Richmond, with Catterick Garrison just up the road.

The origin of the name is from Saint Aubin, a Breton monk who became Bishop of Angers and is remembered for his defence of the weak and oppressed. The Cormier is a local tree which grows to a height of about 15 metres and has pretty white flowers in the spring, pear shaped green fruits in the summer and a richly coloured foliage in the autumn. The fruits are sometimes used to brew beer.

The name 'Richmond' has had fantastic impact on the earth over the last 900 years.

WIKIPEDIA TERMS OF USE

This is a human-readable summary of the Terms of Use.

Disclaimer: This summary is not a part of the Terms of Use and is not a legal document. It is simply a handy reference for understanding the full terms. Think of it as the user-friendly interface to the legal language of our Terms of Use.

Part of our mission is to:

Empower and Engage people around the world to collect and develop educational content and either publish it under a free license or dedicate it to the public domain.

Disseminate this content effectively and globally, free of charge.

You are free to:

Read and Print our articles and other media free of charge.

Share and Reuse our articles and other media under free and open licenses.

Contribute To and Edit our various sites or Projects.

Under the following conditions:

Responsibility – You take responsibility for your edits (since we only host your content).

Civility – You support a civil environment and do not harass other users.

Lawful Behaviour – You do not violate copyright or other laws.

No Harm – You do not harm our technology infrastructure.

Terms of Use and Policies – You adhere to the below Terms of Use and to the applicable community policies when you visit our sites or participate in our communities.

With the understanding that: USE OF WIKIPEDIA

You License Freely Your Contributions – you generally must license your contributions and edits to our sites or Projects under a free and open license (unless your contribution is in the public domain).

No Professional Advice – the content of articles and other projects is for informational purposes only and does not constitute professional advice.

Our Terms of Use

Imagine a world in which every single human being can freely share in the sum of all knowledge. That's our commitment.

Welcome to Wikimedia! The Wikimedia Foundation, Inc. ("we" or "us"), is a nonprofit charitable organization whose mission is to empower and engage people around the world to collect and develop content under a free license or in the public domain, and to disseminate it effectively and globally, free of charge.

To support our vibrant community, we provide the essential infrastructure and organizational framework for the development of multilingual wiki Projects and their editions (as explained here) and other endeavors which serve this mission. We strive to make and keep educational and informational content from the Projects available on the internet free of charge, in perpetuity.

I have always used Wikipedia and must thank them very much for allowing me to use basic facts on Richmonds of the World Book. Many thanks and hopefully Wikipedia will learn something from the ROW Book for other people to enjoy and benefit. BS

ACKNOWLEDGEMENTS/PERMISSIONS RE: TEXT/QUOTES

AUSTRALIAN TOURIST OFFICE
BAHAMAS TOURIST OFFICE
RICHMOND ON LINE (ROL)
MOONBURST
DAVID MORRIS HONOUR OF RICHMOND
HISTORY OF THE EARLS AND DUKES OF RICHMOND
RICHMOND.ORG
VISITRICHMOND
RICHMOND VIRGINIA
NEW HISTORIC RICHMOND TOWN NEW YORK
RICHMOND VANCOUVER
HISTORIC RICHMOND TOWN
RICHMOND CALIFORNIA
RICHMOND INDIANA
RICHMOND TEXAS
RICHMOND VERMONT
JAMAICAN TOURIST BOARD
ST VINCENT AND GRENADINES TOURIST BOARD
GRENADA TOURIST BOARD
GOODWOOD HOUSE
GOODWOOD FESTIVAL SPEED
GOODWOOD RACECOURSE
CARRIBEAN TOURIST BOARD
ENGLISH HERITAGE
RICHMOND CASTLE
MIDDLEHAM CASTLE
ASKE HALL
EASBY HALL
KIPLIN HALL
BOLTON CASTLE
RABY CASTLE
LORDS CRICKET GROUND
AUGUSTA GOLF COURSE USA
WELCOME TO YORKSHIRE
YORKSHIRE RIDINGS
YORKSHIRE LIFE
DALESMAN MAGAZINE
MACKENZIE THORPE
DAVID HODGSON
HAROLD BELL
WIKIPEDIA

BIBLIOGRAPHY

The Swale: A History of the Holy River of St Paulinus by David Morris
The Honour of Richmond: a history of the lords, Earls and Dukes of Richmond by David Morris
Richmond Castle and Easby Abbey
History of Richmond by Mark Whyman

Lightning Source UK Ltd.
Milton Keynes UK
UKOW06f0715210713

214086UK00001B/1/P